"Brittany is a brilliant writer who maste[...] of hardships, heartbreak, and healing. A Dangerous Hope is a beautifully grounded book that you'll have trouble putting down."

— CHELSEA SCOTT
Author and Creator of The Millennial Miss Blog

"Brittany is the epitome of a mother who loves being a mother. Her perspective and advice is groundbreaking. Her wisdom and words are not to be missed."

— LAURA RUTLEDGE
Reporter and Host for ESPN network and
SEC Nation and Former Miss Florida

"What a magical testament this book is to the power and will of hope! Brittany's journey is one so many women can relate to, gain wisdom and hope from, the lessons in this book are invaluable, it is an absolute MUST READ for women at all stages of life."

— SARAH CENTRELLA
Best selling author of Hustle Believe Receive,
#Futureboards and All the Things I Wish I Knew

"Brittany's pure heart shines through in this story of her soul's journey. Women (and men) will be inspired to read her raw words and essentially, the ancient wisdom that is channeled through her."

— MARYN GREEN
Author of Indie Birth

"Some authors give lip service to the topics they talk about but Brittany has the real chops to back up what she says. With wisdom, grace, and loads of authenticity, she tackles topics of motherhood identity, belonging and what happens when life doesn't go the way we thought it would. You'll resonate with every part of her story. You'll laugh with her wit. You'll swim in her wisdom. This is a page-turner you don't want to miss."

— ALLISON FALLON
Author of The Power of Writing it Down

"Vulnerable and refreshing. The way you unpack your life, struggle and faith journey is brutally honest - and it's the kind of transparency this generation needs in order to heal. I've read a lot of people talk about vulnerability, but it's another thing entirely to see a friend live a vulnerable life - and then to share it with us. Reading Brittany's words is just like having a conversation with her - her gift is that she's always looking for the truest, most real thing in life - and in the people around her. These words are her heart in written form, and I'm eternally grateful she's sharing them with a hurting, lost generation."

— TONY ANDERSON
Composer, Filmmaker and
Creator of the Heart of Man Film

"Brittany gets emotionally deep as she shares her personal story of going from the shadows of a small town Kentucky girl to the worldwide stage of being a baseball wife. While the world looked at her with awe, she struggled to find her purpose. She travels to India to help sex trafficking survivors and begins on a spiritual path to reignite her soul and life purpose."

— BRITTNEY KELLEY
Designer, mental health advocate, and
Owner of Tribe Kelley

"Brittany writes with wisdom, authenticity, and honesty. As a sufferer of recurrent pregnancy loss, the words in these pages feel like a warm hug. This book is a must-read for any woman who feels like she's losing hope."

— JORDAN LEE DOOLEY
National Bestselling Author of Own Your Everyday
and Embrace Your Almost

dangerous hope

From Survival Mode to a Wildly Abundant Life

Tony and Brooke -

Thanks for your love &
support. You both shine
so bright. Love you!
Brittany Ross

BRITTANY A. ROSS

Fedd Books
P.O. Box 341973
Austin, TX 78734
www.thefeddagency.com

Published in association with The Fedd Agency, Inc., a literary agency.

ISBN: 978-1-957616-17-9
eISBN: 978-1-957616-18-6

Library of Congress Number: 2022913223

Printed in the United States of America
First Edition 22 23 24 25 /6 5 4 3 2

TABLE OF CONTENTS

DEDICATION

For every little girl who ever felt like she took up too much space.

For every woman that subconsciously runs away from herself. It's time to have hope, heal, and be free.
Awaken, my loves.

Especially, for Gypsy and River.

foreword

THERE IS A COMMON THREAD AMONG PEOPLE WHO HAVE CHANGED THE WORLD. Some may say it's confidence; others may say it's unrelenting resolve. While both hold true, I'm convinced it's the ones who have dangerous hope that leave the world a better place than they found it.

I've heard it said by many that faith is the currency of heaven. We read that it's by people's faith that Jesus couldn't help but marvel, resulting in a breakout of healing. In fact, so much value is placed on pure faith that just a mustard seed will do. So if it's faith that moves mountains, what is hope? It's an interesting concept when you sit down and think about the difference between faith and hope. While I am no theologian, and won't attempt to do an exegesis breakdown on the two concepts, I will strive to communicate that faith dwindles without hope.

Dangerous hope is the prerequisite to authentic faith. Dangerous hope is the soil in which our dreams are buried and the garden in which our suffering is redeemed. Dangerous hope is the fruit of our secret place and the birthplace of our identity. Dangerous hope is the dependence on the

Father and the healthy attachment to the Holy Spirit. But more than any of these things, dangerous hope is the all-consuming and compelling truth that God is faithful.

It transcends dialects and diagnoses. It's the presence of a Heavenly imagination. It's what squeezes joy out of obedience. It's the healing balm to a lonely heart. What I am trying to say is that hope sets us apart because it can't be manufactured or self-sustained. It has to be fought for and cultivated. In a world that praises filters and phony, what stands out more than pure hope?

Odds are that when I mentioned people who have changed the world, someone specific came to mind. Did that person experience trial and pain? Did they persevere through the rough waters of life and live to tell the tale? Yes, of course, they did. Because nobody stumbles into a life of hope. Nobody wakes up successfully avoiding all trauma and suffering only to find themselves with a heart full of hope. Having hope is a war; it's a battle for the heart and the mind. And just when we think it's packaged beautifully, wrapped with a red bow, we will hold it close only to learn the red we see is not of a bow but the blood of a man who conquered death. Because of this blood, we can dangerously hope.

We can weep when the doctor tells us our baby's heartbeat is no longer there. We can lose it when our loved ones leave us, or the scans have come back, and it's stage four cancer. We can grieve the absence of that life-long dream that has been tucked away for several decades because what hope doesn't do is ignore reality and the emotions that come with it. Instead, hope connects itself to the Nature of Jesus – unrushed, open to interruption, deeply committed to delivering peace in a storm. Because true, honest, dangerous hope is the evidence that God is faithful and that our story won't end in ashes.

It is in the deep agony-filled tears of Hannah, believing for a child, that shows me hope moves heaven. It is in the woman who has been bleeding for twelve years that grabs the hem of His robe that shows me hope attracts miracles. It is in the woman who pours her alabaster jar on the feet of Jesus that shows me hope lavishes its treasure on what it values.

Because dangerous hope weeps, reaches, and releases.

When I met Brittney in 2015, I remember immediately noticing something different about her. Our lives, our occupations, our journey into motherhood, and the battles we faced were impossibly similar, and I knew I desperately needed the fruit that flowed from her life. We developed the space within our friendship to confess when hope felt fictional, and faith seemed irrelevant. We spent countless hours mapping out strategies for how we could wiggle out of our circumstances on our own strength. And though we felt we were close a few times, we both came to a conclusion: the Divine Romance.

I have watched Brittany do many incredibly inspiring things with her life. I've seen her pack her bags and leave cities and friends she deeply loved because of her commitment to her husband's career. I've watched her lean into the discomfort of serving the anti-human trafficking industry. I've seen her walk through pregnancy loss time and time again, only to find her continuing to partner with vulnerability. I've watched her navigate the tension of adoption and the broken but beautiful pieces that flow from it. But beyond all these things, the most inspiring moments I've witnessed in Brittany's life have been seeing the remnants of hope refusing to leave, despite the battlefields she finds herself in.

As you turn the pages of this book, maybe you'll find yourself reading familiar stories of trial and pain. When you do, I pray you'll be reminded that dangerous hope rewards those humble enough to search for it and those brave enough to fight for it. When you find yourself holding the sacred prize of hope, I pray you'll look up only to see two hands with holes in them, followed by a voice close enough to whisper, "I'm so proud of you, my hopeful one."

introduction

MARATHONS

WE AREN'T MEANT TO LIVE IN SURVIVAL MODE.

I come from a long line of women who are strong, intelligent, and really good at running from big emotions. I don't actually physically run unless I'm being chased. But when it comes to emotional turmoil, I'm a marathon runner.

Emotional survival was my goal for the first twenty years of my life. God made me extra sensitive. An empath, they call me. Extra touchy—a deep feeler and deep thinker. I used to believe my emotions made me too much for the world around me, so I spent years of my life trying to quiet those emotions to survive without really knowing who I was. I tried my best to bend and shrink myself to fit the roles society and those around me expected me to fit into. I molded my passions to things that were societally acceptable, made sure my beliefs matched the status quo, and that I never rocked the boat too much.

The precarious grasp I had on my identity loosened entirely when I became a "baseball wife." As the wife of a professional baseball player, I found myself navigating social situations I didn't fully understand, missing the mark on expectations that didn't make sense to me, and losing myself more and more each day amid the pressure to meet other people's standards.

If I got caught up in running after all these standards, ideals, and expectations that other people set for me, then I knew I would be too busy to hear the dangerous hope whispering in my soul that there was something more for me. The hope that would take me down unfamiliar paths and hard inclines and test everything I knew.

For so long, I ignored the hope that softly called to the depths of my soul. Instead, I drowned it out by choosing comfort and familiarity and trying to make my life fit a mold that was never made for me. I wanted to hide my emotions, run from them, and use perfectionism to pretend I didn't have them. But now, I know my emotions are a guide. God made them to reveal truths to me. Emotions can be trusted to reveal truths but do not always have to be acted on. Every part of my journey brought my emotions to the surface so that I could truly heal. Truly be free.

That quiet dangerous hope took me to the darkest places in my soul and around the globe itself, but I found who I truly am. I started working with a safe home program in India during one of the darkest seasons of my life. A five-year season of loss after loss and grief piled on top of grief meant I barely knew who I was anymore. From the unexpected loss of my grandma, who was more like a parent to me, to climbing the emotional mountain of becoming a mother, to the crumbling of the religion I once knew, I could barely see the light in my own life.

Little did I know, the catalyst for setting me free, for bringing light back into my own life, would come from seeing inside the darkest industry in the world during my darkest season. Watching young girls heal from the abuse they'd endured as I experienced the depths of personal grief taught me that we are strongest when we hold tightly to the hope of healing and redemption.

Through my story, I pray that you find the courage to stop running emotional marathons too. If you dare to slow down in your pain, you might find hope in the Divine. You might learn to trust yourself again. You might find out that you are wild and free. Lean into the dangerous hope that you were created to heal and stop living in survival mode.

chapter one
WILD FAITH

HAVE YOU EVER MET SOMEONE whose faith felt alive, tangible, and electric? So much so that their faith reminds you of the faith you had but lost in adulthood, trauma, or hardships? If you think back to being a child, before the world told you how to act or who to be, there was a time you were deeply connected to yourself, others, and the Divine.

These people are a rare breed and a bit rebellious if you ask me. They've learned to turn darkness into light. We often think of being rebellious as a negative thing, but the more I look at society, the more I believe a true act of rebellion is to find living faith in a culture obsessed with perfectionism, status quo, and pretending. These rebels are guided by the Holy Spirit, not culture; they are a breath of fresh air. To me, they are like torches that ignite others whose faith is dwindling, dimmed, or dormant like mine was. They are messengers, preparing us for the spiritual journey we are about to embark on, and lighthouses for those of us lost in the storm. I met one such person several years ago.

My husband Robbie (RR for short) and I sat across from Tony and Brooke to discuss their work fighting human trafficking. Since we had been invited to travel to India to check out anti-human trafficking organizations that we might fund, we decided to talk to someone who had a lot of experience in that area. We had visited various non-profits in several other countries. Yet, on that trip to India, we were scouting places where we would learn more about the effect extreme poverty has on human trafficking victims and survivors.

Tony is a musician and a creative. He created and produced the film, *The Heart of Man*, which expressed his heart after his work in anti-trafficking and working with victims of sexual exploitation. It depicts God's love for his children even when we are in the darkest parts of our lives. The film documents prominent thought leaders and individuals like William Paul Young, author of *The Shack*, who became lost in sexual bondage like porn addictions and affairs. And Dan Allender who uncovers that shame is at the root of all mental, emotional, and physical slavery.

I couldn't relate to the stories of a broken marriage or sexual bondage, but I knew very well what it felt like to not feel free, and the hope of his message drew me in—the hope that somehow these people who had seemingly destroyed their lives because of the choices they made found hope and began to rebuild. And they also claimed that the darkness they walked through was the breeding ground of hope. Without the pain, there was no rising.

I knew I was about to walk into one of the darkest industries in the world, but Tony's film reminded me that maybe God wasn't this distant, often disappointed Being, handing out punishments to the sinful. Perhaps, this God would pull up a seat when we're sitting in the dark, stay with us even when we blame Him, and make beautiful things out of the dust.

That kind of hope spoke to me, drew me in, and pushed me forward. So, I went with hope—hope that I'd make it out alive. Hope for human trafficking survivors. And hope for women—the many women I encountered daily who seemed to live in their own chains of darkness.

I'd met Tony a handful of times in college. He never remembered who I was. That both pissed me off and made me more curious about him. Even though we were barely acquainted, Tony and Brooke skipped the small talk. I love that about them. As an Enneagram Four, I always want to go deeper.

"If you really want to work in anti-trafficking," Tony began, "you need to know what nobody else will tell you, and that's that the enemy will come for you. I've had attacks on my life ever since the day I started. It is spiritual warfare at its finest. The enemy is the most offended by people who dare to enter the darkest industry in the world. You need to stay close to God to make it out. And you won't be the same." Tony spoke so confidently, and matter-of-factly, that it almost startled me. I heard his words but didn't understand their gravity until I could look back and see the warfare he was talking about.

The food arrived. And thank God. How do you even respond to something like that? Here I was, about to go to India to visit anti-trafficking projects and potentially get involved in fighting the darkest industry in the world, and this guy said that if I did, I would never be the same. Cool—noted.

I was having trouble keeping up with what Tony was talking about, and then I realized he was actually praying—eyes wide open, hands gesturing all over the place. He looked each of us in the eyes as he prayed a blessing over our lives, asking the Holy Spirit to not only protect us but also to go before us, join us, and show us the way.

Praying had only been done one way: eyes closed, heads bowed, posture tense, addressing God like He was up in the clouds or far, far away, ever wishful that our prayers would reach Him. This was unlike anything I'd seen before. Tony prayed like Jesus wasn't just listening to him but sitting at the table with us.

What is going on? I thought as I awkwardly grinned and set my fork back down. We left dinner hours later. In the car, I waited for RR to say the first word, but he didn't, which was odd. He usually has a lot to say.

"So," I started, "was that the weirdest night you've ever had?"

"Uh, yeah! What just happened?" Robbie asked.

I couldn't tell if he enjoyed our time or was freaked out. Or both.

"Is Tony on drugs?" I asked, slightly joking but also seriously wondering.

"No, I don't think he is. I think he is really just like that."

Robbie and I are from the South, the Bible Belt. If you drive long enough down the interstate, on one side of a billboard, you'll see the words "Turn or Burn" and a Bible verse and on the other side: "Buy one dildo, get one free." Deep in the hills of Kentucky, it's normal to find pop-up snake handling churches and other questionable things. I still hear comments like "women belong in the kitchen."

By this point, I am used to religion which looks a little funny. Sideways, if you know what I mean. Makes you tilt your head a little. But this wasn't just religion that looked a little funny. This was faith lived out. It was different in an amazing, fascinating way.

This was something wild. Real. Contagious. Freeing.

I wanted what Tony had, no matter the cost. I knew it'd be worth it in the end. I just didn't know what was really at stake. Even though RR and I were still nervous, we were also excited to see what our journey to India would bring.

The flights were booked. The visas were ready. There was no turning back.

* * *

"Head down the street three kilometers, take the roundabout, and when you see a goat wearing a blue sweater chained to a pole, then take an

immediate left. There you'll see red doors with gold embellishments—
that's us. That's the safe house."

That's how you give directions in India. Standing in the hotel lobby
with my husband behind me, I listened as Vinita, the director of the safe
home, confidently told the taxi driver how to get to Nai Asha. Nai Asha,
meaning "New Hope" in Hindi, is a project that rescues women and girls
from human trafficking and provides a two-year program that includes
a home, shelter, safety, education, skills training, and love as a holistic
approach to healing from the trauma of sexual abuse and trafficking. Nai
Asha was struggling to survive. Though we visited several other programs
in Northern India, none stood out quite like this one.

As we moved from the hotel to the car, I put my hands together in a
prayer position and bowed my head to the door guard, a man who hadn't
seemed to leave his post in the week since I had arrived in India. "Namaste,"
I repeated. Namaste—meaning the light in me honors and acknowledges the
light in you—was something I was used to saying daily in my yoga practices
in the States. But saying it here in the birthplace of yoga, something that had
brought so much light and joy into my life, gave it extra meaning. The guard
smiled back at me in a way that felt familiar, as if I belonged. The hotel staff
had already asked a few times if I was sure I wasn't Indian.

In every country I'd ever been to—Uganda, Ethiopia, Haiti, and the
Dominican Republic, to name a few—I'd been mistaken as a local. Maybe
that is why I felt more at home with my feet on foreign soil than in my
hometown of Lexington, Kentucky, where my neighbors were also often
confused about where I was from.

I felt more at home in India than I ever had anywhere else.

Perhaps, it was Vinita. She became like a second mother to me. Perhaps
it was the way the Divine made Himself known to me in India in ways I
had longed for my whole life—ways that had eluded me in all my years
going to church, attending a Christian school, spending week nights at

prayer groups, and going on mission trips. Not to mention, the miracles I witnessed were enough to make me fall in love with that part of the world for the rest of my life.

Right before we left for this trip, several doctors told RR not to come. He was diagnosed with an inguinal hernia and told that traveling over twenty-four hours on a plane could make it rupture and would require emergency surgery. I watched my husband's hernia heal after a local pastor and his wife laid hands on him and prayed over him.

It was probably a mix of things that made India feel like home, but I knew that when my feet touched Indian soil, electric energy—rare and sacred— shot through my feet and covered my soul. That covering would follow me through the rest of my journey as I set out on a mission to find myself as a wife, woman, and mother—and ultimately reclaim my rebel spirit.

At this point in life, I had lived several different lives. In one life, I was a girl from Kentucky, a small(ish) town girl. Big morals. Bigger hair. I married my high school sweetheart. While most of my friends from my hometown were graduating college with degrees that they weren't sure how to use, I'd been married for five years, traveled internationally with several different non-profits, and simultaneously wrestled with my body as I tried to get and stay pregnant.

Then there was the baseball life. RR was a pitcher for the Boston Red Sox at the time, so we were living the high life. I had no idea what I was in for when I married a professional athlete. (Of course, when we were in high school, no one had told me he was professional-athlete-level good). I showed up (late) on opening day in 2012 at the Texas Rangers ballpark, where 50,000 fans filled the stadium. I realized, "Dang, this is a pretty big deal, huh?"

Watching RR play baseball at our small high school was about my only experience with sports. So, I was too naive and oblivious to ask what to expect, and RR was too humble to explain things along the way. Essentially, I was completely lost when it came to what was expected of me as the wife of a professional athlete. Learning things the hard way along the way seemed to be my destiny as I stumbled through a brand-new lifestyle in the public eye and messed up—a lot.

I wasn't ready for the extravagant lifestyle off the baseball field: moving three times a year, VIP invites to red carpets, parties, galas, and events, private rooms in restaurants, and more travel than anyone could fathom. The baseball lifestyle isn't something you can understand until you've woken up in a city and not remembered where you are or when you are known better by the TSA agents in the airport than your neighbors. When strangers at my terminal gate made small talk and asked me where I lived, I answered truthfully by saying, "Here, at the airport." Truth be told, the life that came with baseball is a completely separate book in and of itself.

I lived in the public eye because of my husband's career—which added an extra juicy layer of pressure and extreme guilt because I never felt like I fit into my own life. Many people back home knew *of* me, not because of *me*, but because of my husband's career as a professional athlete. But the real question was how could they know me when I didn't even know myself? I spent so much time molding my life to support my husband's career and pursuing his dreams that I didn't know who I really was or have any dreams of my own.

But then came the person I was when I traveled the globe, the me I met in India. This version of me seemed to be the truest—the closest to who I was as a little girl who had a deep trust in the Divine and followed her re-bellious heart. Even though I still didn't feel at home in my own body, being in India was the closest thing I found to having peace. No one knew me in India except a handful of people—and none cared about my church atten-dance, marriage, or status as a "baseball wife."

I found the freedom to be myself without pressure, expectations, or the weight of being married to a baseball player. Suddenly, all the labels that either didn't matter or stressed me out were stripped away. I could just be myself and follow my heart without worrying about how it looked to others. But it wasn't just that I could act like myself without the labels in India. I wasn't in the country long before I realized there was also a purpose for my time there. There was real work to be done, and I was a part of it.

* * *

RR, Vinita, and I squished into the backseat of our cab as we headed to Nai Asha, and we had the whole cab ride to chat. After all, a few kilometers down the road can take a full thirty minutes to an hour in India, depending on traffic.

Vinita started Nai Asha out of a need she had in her own childhood. Vinita is a beautiful, dark-brown-skinned Indian woman with long hair. She has the kind of skin and hair that glows in a way Americans pay money for. But just like in America, prejudice exists in India. Her stepmother considered her too dark-skinned and threw her out of her home as a young girl. She became homeless, vulnerable, and at risk of abuse that came from the hands of disgusting men.

She needed a mother to protect her from abuse, betrayal, and abandonment. At thirty-five years old with two children of her own, she became the mother she'd needed for over three hundred girls who have since graduated from Nai Asha's two-year safe home program that rescues girls from sex trafficking.

Nai Asha was losing its funding, and the girls were going to lose their home, shelter, safety, and hope of creating a new life. When the need arose to partner with Nai Asha, it was an easy yes. But what that meant, we still weren't sure. We originally planned to give a one-time gift. But eventually, a one-time gift turned into a more sustainable and full-time partnership.

We were approaching the safe home, and just like Vinita told our cab driver, the goat was wearing a blue sweater chained to a pole outside the beautiful red doors with gold embellishment.

I walked toward the safe home door and felt the dusty road beneath my feet. I smelled the air that always carries the scent of fire and incense. I took a deep Ujjayi breath to clear my mind and set my intention for the visit. Ujjayi breathing is a therapeutic yogic breathing technique that helps connect you back to your body by breathing in slowly through your nose, pausing, and then out through your mouth. It is also called ocean breathing because you make an oceanic sound in the back of your throat—almost like you are trying to fog up a mirror. It calms the nervous system and helps ground you into the present moment.

That was the opposite of what I did back home. I was in the habit of escaping my mind and body rather than grounding in the moment, always breathing shallow breaths unintentionally. This wasn't purposeful; mentally escaping just happens when you're trying to outrun yourself and your pain. I had learned Ujjayi breathing in yoga years before I knew I would ever find myself in India, using it to stay present and grounded as I talked to survivors of sex trafficking.

We were greeted at the door by the resident girls with singing and sand art on the concrete floor of the entrance. For obvious reasons, they were shy and standoffish on the first day. They wrapped marigolds around my neck. After some time, they began excitedly practicing their English with me as I exchanged the Hindi I knew with them.

I met four of the girls—Ruchi, Maya, Shabnam, and Priya—on their third day at the safe home. They were angry, scared, thin, and looked twice their age. They were noticeably different than the others who had been in the program a year or longer. The other girls were strong; they smiled and had a sparkle in their eyes. They were full of life and joy. By looking at them, you'd never know that just over a year ago, they had been kept in a brothel where they were raped up to fifteen times each day.

Ruchi, Maya, Shabnam, and Priya had bruises, and they barely made eye contact. They were scared, removed, nearly lifeless. The other girls looked like children. The safe house program had worked for them. They were given the environment to heal and come alive. It is amazing what we can heal from when given the right tools and a safe place to flourish. I wondered what it would be like for Ruchi, Shabnam, Maya, and Priya if I saw them again. Would life come back in their eyes? Was it ever too late for some of them?

Ruchi stood to share part of her story in circle time. This was a big deal for her as it would be for any of us. But Vinita told us she was the feisty one. In just three days, she had given them more trouble than any of the other girls combined. She was violent. She'd get up in the middle of the night and beat the others while they were sleeping. The staff thought there was demonic oppression, and they prayed over her daily, which only worsened matters.

"I am thirteen years old. I was trafficked by a family member who abused me since I was little." Ruchi said. "I took the abuse for my little sister so that she wouldn't be abused too. I am worried for her now. She is still with them. I want to leave and protect her."

Tears ran down her cheeks as she spoke. Suddenly, her eyes rolled in the back of her head, and she continued to speak in Hindi. Vinita rushed to her side, held her hand, and prayed in Hindi. Ruchi's body collapsed into Vinita as Vinita continued to pray, and the other girls fanned Ruchi with their hands.

Ruchi started to sweat intensely, and it almost looked like she was having a seizure. I watched nervously, not taking my eyes off the scene. My tears quickly transitioned into fear. What was happening to her? Did she faint? Is this a seizure? Was this demonic oppression?

On our last day in the safe home, the girls came running toward me, giddy, having adopted me as their sister after just one week. "Didi! Didi!" they squealed. Didi means "big sister" in Hindi.

I hugged them tightly, and they wrapped their arms around me, all of us realizing we didn't know when we would see each other again. I held back tears, knowing I couldn't make them any promises. I wanted to, but

I knew better than to position myself as some American hero.

There were a lot of logistics to work out in our partnership with Nai Asha: What would that look like? How often would I travel back and forth? What level of involvement is needed? But we were committed.

* * *

In India, I started seeing myself and my faith come alive. How could it not? This was the beginning of letting go of religion in exchange for faith. The Holy Spirit is wild like that. That dangerous hope whispered in my ear. I was present. I was myself. I had a purpose. But I still had such a long way to go.

Sometimes in life, we need to take a deep Ujjayi breath. We need to practice being present—taking in all our surroundings and embracing the moment we are in. It is hard to find opportunities to pause, especially for those of us living in the confines of American hustle culture. When we are running as fast as we can away from the hard emotions, trauma, and discomfort, we don't have time to catch our breath—much less an Ujjayi breath. Today, in this moment, I encourage you to pause, stop running, stop reading, and take a deep breath—that's how the healing begins.

chapter two

FINDING RENU

THE MONTHLY RESCUE REPORTS I received from Nai Asha revealed the same darkness: abuse, neglect, abandonment, rape, and trafficking, often by a family member. The government was still sending new girls to Nai Asha to heal, but there was a new and pressing issue: lack of funding.

I called Christy, a mentor, and asked for her help in creating a business plan to partner with Vinita and the Director of Operations and Raids at Nai Asha, Ashish—while I filled out paperwork to submit to the IRS so that Mission 108 could become an official NGO (non-governmental organization).

There was a need to be met and that deep maternal instinct kicked in as I was asked to meet it. Having no idea what it meant to create and run a non-profit, I consulted our business manager, lawyers, and other non-profit leaders. Turns out, it takes a lot more effort, time, energy, and funding to start a non-profit than I thought. Nai Asha was worth it, but time was not on our side. With no funds coming in, Vinita, Nai Asha, and their small staff were about to have to close the doors. The girls they had been caring for would be back on the streets of India, where they would likely be trafficked again.

Approval from the IRS can take anywhere from twelve to twenty-four months.

I hired a lawyer who helped us speed up the process, and only a handful of months later, we were approved by the IRS as a legal 501(c)(3) non-profit. Getting approved this quickly was a miracle in itself.

Eventually, I became the American extension of Nai Asha by creating Mission 108, sharing our work, fundraising, educating, empowering, and advocating for victims and survivors of trafficking both in the states and India. While I am not in India on the frontlines, tending to daily needs, I chose to help carry the burden both financially and emotionally with Vinita and Ashish.

My heart shifted from giving a one-time gift to investing in a long-term partnership with Vinita, Ashish, and the girls when I got the call in late 2016 about Renu and heard her story. Renu reminded me that no one is too far from the reach of hope.

Renu wasn't the typical girl rescued. She wasn't rescued from a brothel but a hospital. Vinita got a call about her because she was left for dead in a hospital that didn't even have a bed for her to take her last breath.

The hospital said there was nothing they could do for her. She would pass in weeks, possibly days. They would allow her to stay in the hospital on the floor, but they wouldn't allow her to take up any bed space from the other patients because she was from a lower caste. The caste system in India is their social hierarchy, assigned at birth, which determines a person's rights. The caste system dictates not only your economic status but also your dress, diet, ceremonial observances, and rituals at birth, marriage, and death. It is believed that the only way to move to a higher caste is to strictly obey the governing rules of your current caste so that after you die, you can return to a higher caste. As you can imagine, that system doesn't work out for the poor.

Renu had no money to pay her hospital bills, was ill, and was suffering from neglect and abuse. Someone called Vinita to see if she could help this tiny, fragile four-foot-something girl named Renu, who was on the brink of death.

But Vinita was walking through her own hard season. The funding that was coming from a previous American NGO had ended abruptly, and I was still in the process of creating Mission 108, while she and Ashish were left to provide for thirteen girls. Not only were they running the safe home, providing education, feeding them, clothing them, and giving them love, they were now left with zero funding and support. They were seven months behind on rent. They didn't even have money for food, never mind paychecks. Things were hard.

When they got the call about Renu, Vinita and Ashish had different opinions about whether they could take her in. Ashish was using his critical thinking mind, thinking of the girls they already had and couldn't care for without funding. In his opinion, Renu was probably better off in the hospital. And arguably, she was. He had to consider what burden this would put on the other girls and themselves.

Vinita pushed back. But would the hospital staff love and care for her? Clearly, not. Would they make her comfortable as she went to the other side? Would they step in and intervene to save her life if she showed any signs of a miraculous improvement? Vinita was thinking with her heart as mothers often do.

Neither of them was wrong. Each perspective was important. This is why they make such a great team. Renu was not only an added expense, but she was also a risk. To take her in would mean to love her and open their hearts and wallets up to someone who would pass away in their arms. No matter how long she made it, it would be hard in different ways.

Vinita told Ashish they needed to trust that God would provide. She was no rookie when it came to trusting God to provide when things seemed impossible. Ashish trusted Vinita's wild heart which believed in the impossible, and hoped for miracles.

Vinita had Renu transported from the hospital to the safe home to try to save her life. Within two days of having Renu in the safe home, she started throwing up blood. Vinita was on her way to a funeral when she was told that Renu was not doing well. The staff sent Renu back to the hospital in an ambulance, and Vinita met them there.

When Vinita arrived at the trauma center, the guilt of what she had done came over her. What was all of this going to cost? Was Renu going to die, and would the hospital expect Vinita to cover the expenses? She had no money and was in deep trouble figuring this out. She barely had any money left to her name, as she was using her personal savings to support the thirteen girls in the safe home.

Vinita stayed with Renu in the hospital for one day and one night. As long as she was eating and stable, the plan was to send her to the general hospital upon her release from the emergency room. The general hospital cost was thirty-three Rupees, approximately $.42 USD. Vinita had only twenty-four Rupees in her wallet ($.31 USD). She needed twelve more Rupees to get care for Renu. She asked for help around the hospital, hoping someone could loan her a few cents to get care for this poor, hurting girl.

Not one person would give her the twelve Rupees.

She went to the ATM to attempt to get money. But the minimum withdrawal amount was 1,000 Rupees ($13 USD). Vinita had 586 Rupees in her checking account. (about $7.50 USD). She walked from midnight to two in the morning to find an ATM with a lower minimum so that she could withdraw all her money to make Renu more comfortable as she passed away. Two miles away, she found an ATM that would allow her to withdraw the 596 Rupees. She walked back to the hospital, and at 4 a.m., they released Renu to general care.

Vinita always mentions that everyone who comes to Nai Asha will be blessed. After all, the name of the safe home is New Hope. So, when it came to Renu, everyone knew that if anyone could save her, it was Vinita. I actually believe it is proximity to Vinita that is the blessing. Her presence is heavenly. She exudes a calmness that reflects her hard-earned faith in the Divine. Hard-earned because her faith was not like that of Christians I knew back home. It was that of a woman who had lived the impossible many times, so much so that she believed in a God that performs miracles. And it was because of Vinita that Renu would get a second shot at life—a new hope in a life that wasn't filled with trauma, abuse, and abandonment. In general care, Renu started to make an unexpected turnaround. She was eating and drinking and was stable and able to be released.

Vinita brought her back to life and back to the safe home, where she assumed the prestigious role of boss around the safe house. A miracle, indeed.

After hearing Renu's incredible story of deliverance, I couldn't walk away just because things felt too heavy to carry. I would forever be changed by the hope Vinita had (and gave me) in saving Renu's life. Though I had zero experience running a non-profit and zero intention of ever starting one, if sustainability was the goal and walking in a relationship with people leads to healing, I had to be a part of it. Thus, Renu became the heartbeat behind Mission 108.

I met Renu on my second trip to India. Although she walked with a limp and was missing a finger on one of her hands, she commanded the entire room. She stood barely over four feet tall, wore her hair short, and had her nose pierced like mine. When she smiled, her cheeks covered her eyes, making them like slender crescent moons.

Some of the new girls were hesitant to approach me. Even though my mocha brown skin matched theirs, they were wary of new people—understandably so. I was a strange American to them, and it was only normal to be hesitant. But it only took minutes for them to warm up. Not Renu, though. She walked up to me with authority, like she was trying to make a statement. And she did.

I bent down to meet her at eye level and said, "Hi. You must be Renu. I've heard a lot about you. You are the warrior."

Because of Renu, I carry the burden and the privilege of caring for fifty to one hundred vulnerable girls rescued from trafficking every year. I am invested in their healing. I have the burden and privilege of creating sustainable solutions for their long-term success. Once the girls enter the safe home, they are family forever—if they will have us.

She leaned in, and I cupped her face in the palm of my hands and pressed my forehead against hers. We both closed our eyes and took each other in. She grabbed my hand and led me around as if it were my first time there. Not much about the bones of the safe home had changed, except for the newer girls I was eager to get to know.

The girls followed Renu and showed me their rooms, beds, school area, and new sewing machines they'd been working with. Learning skills and developing trade is a part of the two-year program, which also includes a full education. The girls I met on my first trip were moving to the part of the program where they felt safe and strong enough to focus on their education and explore what jobs they wanted to have after they completed the program. They were excited to practice their English and tease me about my Kentucky-accented attempt at Hindi.

My emotions were swirling as I turned on a hot shower back at my hotel after a long day in the safe home. I stepped into the hot water, already feeling the guilt of getting to wash off the dirt and sweat from the day. Being a privileged American always weighs heavy on my spirit. But what I wrestled with in those moments in the shower was not how little the girls have but how much they do have. I have things, money, access, and education. They have an incomparable joy, light that beams out of them and is infectious, community, and authentic relationships.

Who is rich, and who is poor? They have so little and yet have so much. They are rich in spirit, which is what I wanted. But is that only accessible in a life of deep trauma, pain, and heartache?

My five-star Indian hotel with marble floors and a warm cozy bed suddenly felt like guilt wrapped in a wool blanket on a hot summer day. I let the water hit my back and closed my eyes as my hair fully absorbed the water, making the smell of incense and fire even more pronounced.

The weight of what the girls experienced before the safe home pressed on my shoulders. Soon enough, I couldn't tell the difference between the shower water running down my face and my tears as I bawled like a baby.

Just as my tears washed away in the water, so did my naivety about the world. I was two feet in; no turning back. It wasn't just a one-time gift and a shallow short-term mission trip anymore. It's one thing to hear about human trafficking on the news or in reports, but it's another to hold space for a victim as she cries tears the size of an ocean while I hold her hands and want to take all her pain away but can't. Once you know what I know and see what I've seen, you cannot simply look away. Wouldn't that make me just as evil as those who sit back and do nothing while knowing girls all over the world are trapped in abuse? It is a privilege to carry this burden because to whom much is given, much is expected. But the burden is heavy and many, many times I have wanted to lay it down.

There is a particular kind of darkness that makes you wonder about the condition of the human heart. What causes a person to rape and abuse a child? Is there any ounce of humanity left in someone like that?

I stood in the shower and replayed the stories I'd just heard from the girls. All different but all so grossly and uncomfortably similar. Raped fifteen times in one day but also starved, beaten, and locked in a dark room alone, waiting for the next abuser to come in and have their way with her. Sold by her mother to strangers for pennies.

Raped. Not once. Not twice. Fifteen times a day every day for years.

My body tensed. I bent down and held my face in my hands, crying out for mercy for our girls and the millions whose names I would never know. I couldn't fathom the pain, but I felt the heaviness that this wasn't just something that happened to one girl. It happened to all of them.

My own fears started to rise in my throat. Fears of abandonment, neglect, and the world not being a safe place. Fears that every woman has had living in this cold, hard world. Our minds go there when we are alone in Ubers, walking to the parking lot in the dark, or cat-called by men who've never had to pay the price for their words or actions. But that is the thing, they have only ever been fears in my head.

The girls, just babies really, lived a reality that I had only ever feared or seen on TV. The world is a much darker place than I could have imagined. I wondered: Where are the good men? The protectors?

Where was God?

They say we have a relationship with God the same way we have relationships with our earthly fathers. That made sense to me, as mine wasn't there most of my childhood. He was serving in the military and putting country over self, but there was another price to pay: Me. A relationship with me. We built one when I became an adult. But his absence shaped so much of my view of the world, even though I knew my father loved me and would go to the ends of the earth to protect me.

To me, God was just as absent and mysterious as He'd ever been. At just twenty years old, when I married RR, I was certain I wouldn't marry him or any man who was interested in the military. In my young mind, the military took my dad from me. And while I didn't marry a military man, I also didn't choose a man with a career that made him more present. While RR's life wasn't on the line serving our country, he was gone just as much.

My fears of abandonment and emotional neglect rose as I stepped outside the shower that never ran cold. If I felt this way in my own life, that was pretty cushy, I couldn't even dream of what the girls at Nai Asha felt.

One of the questions I had pondered so much within the past year was, "Is it even possible to heal from this?" But after meeting Renu, knowing where she came from and where she was now, I started to believe that maybe hope had played a part in her healing. Nai Asha proved that healing was very much possible for anyone, including myself. So much has changed in the last year for me. It had been, without question, the darkest year of my life, and I felt like I was fighting for my own soul. I would have never guessed that in this place, surrounded by women and girls who survived horror after horror, I'd find hope and a connection to the Divine, unlike anything I'd ever known.

chapter three

THE PLUS SIGN

TWO YEARS EARLIER

BEFORE I HAD BEEN TO India at all, in 2015, I was invited to Uganda by an organization partnering with the Boston Red Sox—the team my husband was playing on at the time—to fund a project that empowered women living in extreme poverty. One week before I was scheduled to leave for Uganda, I got the surprise of a lifetime. And that surprise was the beginning of my unraveling.

I was sitting in the team doctor's office where the nurse was administering the slew of vaccines recommended for travel. As she pulled the first needle out of my arm, ready to give me the next one, she asked me if I was pregnant or trying to get pregnant.

Something about her question made me feel uneasy. Even though I was a sexually active, married woman, I was still completely unaware of my own ovulation, so I told her no, I was not pregnant or trying to get pregnant. And that was the truth. At least, partly.

The appointment was quick. She told me that my arm might feel sore but that the vaccine had little to no side effects, and then she handed me my prescriptions for malaria medication. I walked out of the office and headed toward the pharmacy. When I got there, the line for the pharmacy was longer than I anticipated. Knowing I would be late for RR's game that night and not really wanting to wait, I turned down the next aisle and decided I would fill the prescription another day. I still had about a week until departure.

As I headed toward the exit, I walked down the aisle with the pregnancy tests. For reasons I'll never understand, something about the nurse's pregnancy question and being in that pharmacy aisle turned my subconscious thoughts into conscious ones. I started wondering if I was pregnant. RR and I weren't trying, but it was certainly possible. We both wanted to be parents but weren't looking to start our family right then. So, I couldn't possibly be pregnant, right? I tried to push the thought out of my mind, but something kept bringing me back to the question: But what if you are pregnant? Don't you want to find out?

I was standing in the aisle with my eyes directed toward the pregnancy tests, staring into space. Just to ease my mind, I bought a test. I had been in that aisle hundreds of times before, buying tampons month after month. Never once had I thought about buying a pregnancy test, but something in my gut was telling me I needed to buy one today. I listened to my intuition, but even as I was checking out, I didn't really know why I bought it. I didn't feel pregnant.

As soon as I walked in our rental house for the season, I raced upstairs and took the test.

While I waited for something to show up and tell me if I was pregnant or not, I thought about becoming a mother. We had been married for five years at this point, and time had passed by with lightening speed. We got married when I was twenty years old. A baby, really. Surviving on nothing but love. Without legally being able to drink at my own wedding, only a handful of years later, I was starting to consider that I might be responsible for another human life in nine short months.

I still had so many questions about life. Like how people even decide when they are ready to become pregnant. Well, in my case, life decided for me. As one dark pink line appeared on the stick, and then another faint pink line appeared, I grabbed the test's box to read the directions. I didn't even know how to decode the thing. There was a diagram indicating where the results window, absorbent tip, and thumb grip were.

"But how the heck do I know if I am pregnant?" I mumbled out loud to myself, hoping my sister-in-law—who was living with us at the time—didn't hear anything going on. I hadn't told Robbie that I had bought a pregnancy test yet. I was already annoyed with myself because I didn't think this whole thing through. Would he be happy? Would he be mad that I didn't wait to do this with him? We do everything together; doing this without him felt a little like a betrayal. The thought of his reaction made me sick to my stomach. Or was that pregnancy nausea?

I was sweating and flustered that I had gone twenty-five years of life not knowing when a woman—myself in particular—ovulates and how to read a pregnancy test.

Then, I saw it:

TWO PINK LINES = PREGNANT

ONE PINK LINE = NOT PREGNANT

I blinked twice and rubbed my eyes. *Was I imagining the second line?* I could hear my heart beating and feel my armpits getting sweatier. The second line was lighter than the first one. *What does that mean?*

I did what every twenty-something, naive woman does in the face of not knowing something. I googled it.

Dr. Google told me quickly that I was, in fact, pregnant.

Nearly everything after that moment was a blur. I know I told Robbie. I know it was a day game, so he was home around dinner. I didn't want to send the news in a text, so I waited for him to get home. When I told him, he didn't believe me. So, he went to the store the next morning and bought five more tests. He was smart enough to buy the ones that actually say "pregnant" or "not pregnant." And while a few tests read negative, enough of them said I was pregnant that RR and I started to get excited. We were going to have a baby.

I'd always wanted to be a mother. When RR and I got married, we made a five-year plan like young kids do, expecting our lives to go as exactly as we wanted. We would wait five years after we got married to start having children both biologically and through adoption so that we could travel the world, mature, and pursue professional baseball without the stress of starting a family and balancing the intense demands of his career.

From the start, we were certain we wanted a big family of both biological and adopted children. RR is one of six, and I am an only child. We had just talked about how our five-year anniversary was approaching. We both mentioned waiting another year or so to get settled in our new baseball city, as he had just been traded to Boston from the Texas Rangers.

But when I found out I was pregnant, there was no turning back.

There is no stronger desire in the world than when a woman has her heart set on motherhood. Hearing your baby's heartbeat only makes that desire and connection stronger.

Through all that excitement and planning, I had to look in the short-term. Was I going to go to Uganda, Africa, the following weekend, or would I cancel my trip? Very thoughtfully and prayerfully, I decided to go to Uganda. *Women are pregnant in Africa all the time,* I thought. Plus, God gave me a vision of a pregnant woman I would meet on my trip, and I took that as a sign that I was meant to go and that everything would be okay.

I was sick and tired the entire week. But it was on that trip that I learned about human trafficking. If I look back at the breadcrumbs that led me to where I am today, that trip, and the conversations I had with the organization I traveled with, introduced me to the reality of human trafficking. Because of that trip, I was invited to India to learn more about trafficking and see some of the projects firsthand.

Even though there was evidence of the Divine written all over it, it would take years to have it revealed to me that nothing about my decision to go to Africa or be in Uganda had anything to do with what happened next. And it would take years for me to stop blaming myself.

Still, to this day, I shudder thinking about it. But ten weeks after I saw my first positive pregnancy test, after traveling to Uganda and back again (then to New York, Detroit, and Miami for baseball, and then to Kentucky to share my pregnancy news with family), things changed forever. I woke up one morning later than usual. I felt crampy and tired and noticed that my other pregnancy symptoms weren't as strong. I wasn't nauseous. My boobs weren't sore. I had a morning appetite. I was ten weeks pregnant, so I made the naive assumption that I was feeling the second trimester boost so many women talk about, just a little earlier than usual.

The pace of my life was a direct reflection of the state of my body: chaotic and disconnected. I was too exhausted to notice what was really happening or where I even was emotionally and mentally. I never sat still long enough to be in the present moment or give my body what it need-ed. While I no longer blame myself for what happened, I do regret that I didn't notice the warning signs, my body's cry for help and that I naively took pharmaceuticals without understanding the risks. Sometimes, when you ignore the body long enough, it will start speaking to you louder and louder until, eventually, everything falls apart.

When I woke up that morning with cramps, I wasn't worried. I didn't expect pain in my life: I was still deceived by the idea that if you were a good Christian woman, you could avoid most pain—even this kind of pain.

But then I started to bleed. I was spotting dark brown blood at first, which my trusty pal Google told me was common in the first trimester. Relief from reading that cramps or bleeding were normal gave me a few hours of mental comfort and distraction.

I was so good at distracting myself. Before this, even though I can see things differently now, my body had worked relatively well for me. I was young, active, and "healthy." Looking back, I can see that my body had been trying to get my attention for years. From the headaches that turned into life-altering migraines, the heavy, painful periods that doctors continuously told me were "normal," and the anxiety, I can see now that my body was always trying to get my attention.

Our bodies are incredible at giving us clues as to what we really need. But when we don't listen, like in my case, and give it the tools it needs, the body will start screaming in ways we never even fathomed. The tools my body needed were not a life of constant travel, fueled by caffeine, using pharmaceuticals without researching or understanding the side effects, or getting "my best rest" on an airplane.

The period-like cramps intensified, and the spotty bleeding turned to bright red like a period. I called RR to let him know that something wasn't right. Just the day before, I wasn't having any of these symptoms.

"I think I need to go to the hospital. There is a lot of blood, and I am in a lot of pain," I told him as I held back tears and forcefully swallowed the lump in my throat.

"Do you want me to meet you there or come home? I need to talk to the manager, but just tell me what you need," he said.

What I need? I thought without giving him an answer. I didn't know what I needed. I was too scared to tell him what I wanted him to do and perhaps too afraid to admit it myself. Deep down, I knew what was happening. What I needed was for someone to make all of this go away. I wanted him to hear in my voice how scared I was and make a choice for me without having to ask for help. I still had so much good Christian girl programming, the kind that didn't allow for any needs deep within me. Better to suffer in silence than to expose my human condition. Even when I knew something could be very wrong, I was worried about being an inconvenience.

He called the team doctor and was instructed to get me to the emergency room as soon as possible. He let the Red Sox management know what was happening, and they told him to leave immediately. This was a shock to both of us, considering baseball players are only given three days of paternity leave when their children are born. Baseball players skip weddings and funerals and plan babies and births around the season.

By the time I got to the ER, I was losing so much blood that I wasn't able to walk. A nurse met me at the door with a wheelchair to take me back to a private room for an ultrasound. And RR got there soon after me. At that point, I wasn't able to talk through the level of pain that came and went like waves, so I was thankful RR was there to talk for me.

After I was in the room and up on the table with my legs spread and feet in stirrups, a nurse greeted me with kind eyes. "We are going to insert this and find the baby's heartbeat," the nurse said calmly. The fact that she seemed to have hope in a heartbeat while knowing that my symptoms gave me comfort amid the intense pain.

Maybe it's an ulcer, I thought. I had been traveling a lot. I was thinking of all the ways this couldn't truly be happening. *There was a healthy baby inside my belly just a few weeks ago. We saw and heard the heartbeat. I have ultrasound pictures to prove it.*

The nurse inserted the vaginal ultrasound stick. The cramping intensified for a moment or two and then washed away, almost like the cramps never even happened. I distracted myself by searching the ultrasound screen for my baby.

"Sometimes they hide. Let's look on the other side." As she moved the vaginal ultrasound stick around and around, the pain returned with even more force. She typed something into the computer but said nothing.

I tried to catch her eyes, but she avoided me. I looked around the room. It was cozier and quieter than most emergency rooms. This was one of the best hospitals in the world, and if anyone could save my baby, it was them. I was still holding onto a naive kind of hope that was more like denial.

She pulled the wand out, and blood like a river rushed from me onto the table and streamed toward the floor. I apologized for the mess when found my voice. She called another nurse in and said, "Let's see if we can get a doctor in here. We need you to stay laying down."

The energy shifted. Robbie and I were both silent, avoiding our reality. Another woman walked in and introduced herself by showing her credentials, which at this point meant nothing to me. "Do you know your blood type?" she asked.

Feeling embarrassed about how naive I had been up to this point in life, the question only brought more shame. I felt like I should know this kind of thing as a woman who wanted to bring a baby into the world. I wanted to be the perfect mom to my unborn baby—and I was failing. I answered her question about my blood type with a simple no but darted my eyes at RR and made a mental note to ask him later if people are supposed to know these kinds of things.

She explained that I was having a miscarriage and losing a lot of blood. "We couldn't find the heartbeat. Sometimes these things happen."

And just like that, everything I was scared to say out loud was confirmed. I was miscarrying. The baby I held in my womb for ten weeks—who I loved, adored, wanted, and prayed for—was gone. My heart hurt. My womb hurt. My entire body hurt from the tension. I just wanted to leave—this hospital, this body, this reality—and go back to my bed and disappear.

That loss led me to question everything. My religion. My identity. My purpose. My womb. My ability to be a good wife. And eventually, question whether I was worthy of being a mother.

Even though I was deep in darkness and pain, I was able to stay curious about the Divine and creation, and I held on to hope in the heartache. Hope looked nothing like I thought it would or like people told me it would.

My curiosity about who God is and if He loves us led me to Uganda, India, and Nai Asha, where there was no denying the evidence of the Divine. Those experiences anchored me as I faced even more loss. Of course, witnessing that level of darkness and evil led to its own set of questions, like why God allows bad things to happen to good people. But I couldn't deny that God was rescuing the girls at Nai Asha, not just from brothels and human trafficking rings, but from the darkness that stayed within them after they were brought to the safe home. They were brought out of the darkest industry in the world into safety, security, and restoration. Dry bones were coming alive right in front of my eyes. Souls were restored. A new hope, indeed. And as I was healing from the loss and heartbreak of my miscarriage, I couldn't help but feel some hope that if God could rescue those women and girls from the darkness of human trafficking, maybe God could rescue me from my darkest season too.

chapter four

DEATH, WHERE IS YOUR STING?

I SAT IN THE EMERGENCY room, my ears ringing as I fumbled through questions like "How could this happen?" and "What does this mean?" and directed the weight of my sadness and confusion over my miscarriage at the nurse who had been with me since she picked me up at the entrance with the wheelchair. She had kind eyes, but I could tell this kind of thing didn't faze her. She was used to it. I didn't say much to her, but I felt a strange comfort being under her care.

When I stood from the table and attempted to walk toward the door to leave, I hurled over from a wave of pain that was stronger than the rest. Things were increasingly getting more intense, and the blood was everywhere.

The kind nurse grabbed my arm and said, "We are going to put you back in this wheelchair."

My stubbornness was showing because I hoped to walk off the pain or pretend to be stronger than I was. Yes, the pain doubled me over, but the continued bleeding sat me back down.

I blinked my eyes intentionally to try to see through the darkness invading my vision. I didn't dare tell anyone I was blacking out. My lips were dry, and I anxiously bit the insides of my cheeks. My body had never betrayed me like this before. I was training to become a yoga instructor then, so I tried to remember how to breathe through the pain. Nothing worked. I was already overtaken by the weight of my loss, the intensity of my pain, and the terror of losing that much blood.

I had never heard anyone say the word "miscarriage" before. My mother-in-law had six children and talked about pregnancy like it was the most beautiful time of her life. She lost a baby around eighteen weeks, but I didn't know about him until I had a loss of my own. The other baseball wives boasted about getting pregnant on their honeymoon or right after they got off birth control. At the time, I didn't know anyone who'd had a miscarriage. Or admitted it. My mom, grandma, and aunt had never spoken about miscarriages or having trouble sustaining a pregnancy. *Why was I so different from them? What was wrong with me?*

I asked the nurse what I was supposed to do next. Of course, she thought I was asking literally, but I wanted to know how or if there was a way to save the baby. I still hadn't accepted what a miscarriage really meant.

She explained that the next two weeks would be completely focused on rest. She asked if I could take off work or if my lifestyle would allow me to easily commit to rest. The thought of not being on the go or traveling made me anxious, but at the same time, this felt like the permission slip I secretly knew I needed. I'd been exhausted for so long, wondering what caused it.

"Um," I stuttered, not knowing how to explain my strange life. I was constantly on the go. How was I supposed to stay in one place and rest for two entire weeks?

She looked at me with soft, kind eyes and said matter-of-factly, "I am so sorry. We don't always have answers for why things like this happen.

And unfortunately, due to insurance, we do not do any follow-up testing until you have had three miscarriages or have been trying to get pregnant for a year."

Her directness comforted me, but at the same time, I couldn't shake the echo of her words: three miscarriages. "Three miscarriages," I repeated quietly. My jaw was locked, and my shoulders were creeping up toward my ears. The tension in my body was building. I could hear her talking, but I wasn't listening.

Three miscarriages.

Three miscarriages.

Three miscarriages.

I couldn't get "three miscarriages" out of my head but snapped back to the present moment to cut her off and interrupt. "Three miscarriages seems like a lot."

"It is. I am so sorry. The good news is you are super fertile after a miscarriage."

I tucked that information away into my subconscious as I sent a mental threat to God that I better not have two more miscarriages.

As the doors slid open, the chilly Boston summer air hit me in the face. I had lost track of time, unsure of how long I had been in the emergency room. It was still light outside, and the sun was setting. This was usually my favorite time of the evening.

But at that moment, my mind and body filled with rage, anger, and fear. Rage and anger that this could be happening to me—the good Christian girl. Fear that these kinds of things happen and are beyond our control. I wondered if it was safe for me to go home, losing this much blood. *This couldn't get any worse.* Time was standing still, and no matter how hard I tried, I couldn't escape my reality.

"I am anemic," I said as I got into the truck, feeling dizzy from the blood loss.

I heard the nurse reminding RR that I would need to go back to see my doctor in two weeks to make sure my uterus was clear. She told RR to watch my bleeding because I could hemorrhage. "If she soaks blood through a pad in less than an hour or two, you must come back in."

I didn't say anything, but I was already soaked. With my history of running away from and shutting down when big uncomfortable emotions like anxiousness, grief, and anger come, its my survival strategy to try to remain in control. I thought not saying anything would give me control over my situation.

Nothing the kind nurse said could have prepared me for the pain and devastation that followed. All the way home and into the night, I went in and out of consciousness, blacking out from the pain and the sadness. Each time I blacked out, I wondered if I would wake up. I was too exhausted to make any real effort to tell RR that I loved him and that I was sorry for losing our baby.

Despite experiencing this intense pain, I was still not focusing on my own well-being but on how others felt. Why do we, as women, do this to ourselves?

RR moved me from the couch where I landed as soon as we got home to my bed. I had no memory of getting there. But I do remember him stroking my hair and staring down at me with intense love.

"Do you need anything? Can I get you anything?" he asked, fear coming through in his tone.

I wanted to tell him everything was going to be okay. But I couldn't get any words out, and even if I could, I was certain they would be a lie. *Nothing was okay.*

Around 3 a.m. I shifted from half-asleep to wide awake; my pain had decreased significantly. For a moment, I thought it was all a nightmare. My body felt so weak, and remnants of the earlier pain quickly reminded me this wasn't just a dream.

It was terrifying to feel so out of control of my body, from the intense bleeding to needing so much help from Robbie. This was all so humbling. I had always thought I was so strong and confident in my ability to do whatever I set my mind to. And yet here I was, having lost a pregnancy that, while unplanned, was very much wanted and basically bleeding to death on my couch and in my bed. I felt like I was failing as a wife and as a woman.

I am having a miscarriage. Some sense of acceptance began to sink in. There is something wild about grief and intense sadness. It grounds us in the present moment almost like no other emotion. Even though we want to escape, we can't. We are right there in our bodies—exactly where we don't want to be.

I got up and tiptoed to the bathroom. As soon as I sat down on the toilet, an urge to push came over me. I gasped for breath in a bit of shock—the nurse had not prepared me for this feeling. I stood up from the toilet instinctively. With one hand, I grabbed the side of the wall and, with the other, quickly grabbed the magazine on the floor to catch whatever was coming out of me.

Within seconds, a tennis sized ball of tissue fell onto the magazine I was holding. A mason jar full of water sat on the sink next to the toilet, so I quickly emptied it and dumped the tissue from the magazine into the mason jar. For me, something didn't feel right about flushing what remnants of my pregnancy and my baby I had left down the toilet.

I could barely look at the jar. I cleaned myself up and reached for my phone. Then I googled, *What does a baby look like at ten weeks pregnant?* My intuition was right. I had just pushed out my placenta and remaining fetal tissue.

Sitting back down on the toilet, I lowered my face to my hands and wept.

In the weeks of pain following my miscarriage, it would have been natural to return to the basics of my family, religion, and my life with RR. But I felt like each of those was crumbling—and had been for some time.

The miscarriage wasn't the first major loss I experienced that year. My Gran had passed that year, several months before I first found out I was pregnant. I thought the pregnancy was a surprise sent to me by my Gran to help me through the grief of losing her. Like a gift from heaven.

How naive.

It felt grimly appropriate that the day I miscarried was also August 19, Gran's birthday, and the first since her passing. To put it plainly, my Gran's death was the beginning of my unraveling. Losing her broke my heart and knocked me off my feet so profoundly that I found it more difficult to continue chasing the image of that perfect Christian girl after her death. It felt pointless to work so hard to please others and pretend like I was okay.

Pretending is too much work for anyone—especially the hurting. There would be no more pretending. I was entering a long stretch of life filled with pain and plenty of space to think about Gran's death and this miscarriage. The grief that follows a miscarriage is dark and confusing, and gut-wrenching. That grief only felt heavier after losing the baby on my Gran's birthday.

Gran was more than a grandparent to me. She was another mother figure. Because my dad was overseas with the military most of my childhood, my Gran was like a parent.

When I got the phone call from my mom—who found my Gran's unconscious body on the bathroom floor—my world turned upside down. RR and I were on our way to a wedding in Knoxville, Tennessee, excited to celebrate the joining together of two lives and to enjoy the rare occasion that we could attend a wedding together. It was a baseball couple, and they had planned their wedding around baseball season as we all do.

When the phone rang, my mom was on the other end, quiet yet hysterical in a way I had never heard her before. I knew something was wrong. And I felt my heart beating faster and faster as she tried to get the words out. The sound of her voice sent chills down my spine. This was not how it was supposed to happen.

Death—that is.

Unable to revive my Gran, my mom called 911. Gran wasn't that old; she wasn't sick or showing any signs that it was the end. She was texting me just a few hours before. It didn't make sense for her to die when she did.

We never made it to the wedding that day. It was a slow, three-hour trip back to the driveway of my mom's house to meet my family. For us, that day would never be about the joining of two lives but about losing one.

We have such little control during our lives, but I'm convinced we have no control of when we take that first and last breath. Birth and death are fated. It is simply not up to us. At least not in our primary consciousness.

* * *

For the first time in my life, I felt the unbearable and radical separation that is heaven and earth. My religion had taught me that if you are a Christian, death loses its sting. Yet here I was, after losing my Gran and my baby, death didn't just sting—losing my baby made me question everything.

I am not certain it was ever said directly, but in the South—especially in Kentucky—it is implied that good Christian girls grow up, get married, and have babies. That is just our role here on earth. Unless you're from the South or a part of this particular Christian culture, you might not fully comprehend the pressure put on good southern Christian girls.

I call this culture "Country Club Christianity"—the CCC. Country Club Christianity is everything you imagine to be. It's the culture of wealthy, religious, conservative Christians widespread in this part of the Bible Belt. As within any social club, there are rules. Some of those rules are written but even more are not. Being a part of that club means you follow the rules and do not dare to question them. If you abide by the rules and pay your dues, you are welcomed into the club. Everyone is welcome to join the club, but you wouldn't feel welcome unless you look, act, and speak like everyone else. Everyone outside of the club knows this, but those inside pretend like they don't. There are many perks and benefits to being a part of the club, and the privilege of being a part of CCC only makes things easier for you.

But the cost of being a part of the club is keeping up with the status quo. Even if it means sacrificing your soul. Eventually, if you aren't actually perfect, your humanity catches up to you. Either you keep up the act of perfectionism, or you are judged, exposed, and your position in the club might be threatened altogether.

There are many hallmarks of the CCC: one of them is what's known as the "Proverbs 31 woman." This metaphor is set before women and, along with the rest of the CCC teachings, sets women up to think that our lives begin and end with the men we marry and the babies we carry. And if we don't get married or the marriage falls apart, or worse, we can't become mothers—we aren't *good*. What does that mean about our worth as humans? If I was going to be like the good, Christian, southern women back home but couldn't keep my pregnancy, what did that say about me as a woman?

I was about to find out.

I was a part of the CCC, and it was a big part of my life. But the more I leaned into my grief, the harder this culture was to be a part of, and the harder it was to keep up the act. When people in CCC asked how I was doing, I made the mistake of telling them the truth.

"When are you and Robbie Ross gonna start having kids?" I'd tell them I was pregnant for ten weeks and just miscarried. Their faces said it all, but they'd always follow up with some well-meaning but hurtful words: "Everything happens for a reason," or worse, "Oh, just have faith. It will happen in God's timing."

If faith could have saved my baby, it would have.

CCC doesn't know what to do with me now, a woman no longer willing to hide parts of herself that God calls important. And from what I can tell, there are many, many more of us waiting for permission to live in such a way that we don't have to spend our lives apologizing for our humanity but instead show up in our skin, fully alive and admittingly human.

Country Club Christianity worked out for me then. After the miscarriage, it didn't. It's not that I always disagree with the message CCC preaches, it's that I don't always align with the energy behind it. (At first, to be honest, I didn't feel like I fit much of anywhere anymore). There is a difference between reading the Bible like a recipe book as opposed to a love letter. The first comes with an undercurrent of shame-based teaching. The latter is like dancing with the Divine. Instead of trying to impress God, you get to be free with Him.

As I wrestled with all of this, I wasn't sure what box to check for religion anymore.

All I knew in the moment was that I had fundamentally changed. Before the miscarriage, I was just a good Christian girl, hiding her rebellious soul by checking all the boxes. I was experiencing great loss, pain, and grief for the first time. That first pregnancy was unplanned but certainly not unwanted. And it sparked a soul-deep desire for motherhood. Of course, now that I wanted to become a mother—a reality that, in a matter of moments, was taken away from me—I not only grieved my pregnancy and losing a baby, but I also grieved the loss of an entire purpose and identity.

I didn't know who I was at all.

Something intense had awoken in me: the desire to become a mother. I had become a lioness chasing her prey; a thirst that could not be quenched until my I had what my heart was set on: motherhood.

chapter five

WHO ARE YOU?

"I WANT TO NAME THE baby, Robbie. Will you pick a name?" I said to Robbie the morning after I miscarried.

I could feel RR's eyes widen as he realized what I was asking him to do, making our loss feel even more real. He didn't know it yet, but I had already snuck downstairs and put the mason jar in the freezer. I fully realized that I might be going crazy—but what else was I supposed to do? I had already decided to catch my own placenta and fetal remains in a mason jar. Naming our baby felt tame in comparison. I wondered to myself, *What do other women who miscarry do? Why is no one talking about this? Am I the only one?*

When I Googled what a ten-week baby in utero looked like, I was displeased to find out that a nearly formed, thumbnail-sized baby had been living inside my body just forty-eight hours earlier. Unfortunately, Google doesn't tell you what steps to take to grieve your pregnancy and miscarriage, so I went with my intuition and just did what felt right, even though I realized it might look a bit crazy. The horrible part was that in several weeks when baseball season was over, and we had to drive twenty hours home, I had to figure out what I was going to do with our mason jar.

I took a deep breath while sitting on the edge of my bed and looked up at him, hoping he would realize how serious I was about naming the baby.

"I want to name the baby," I repeated, looking him square in the eyes with my eyebrows raised slightly. He knew what that eyebrow raise meant after five years of marriage. It communicates a thousand words in one look. It says, "Please don't question me on this. I might lose it." And I was losing it. I was on the brink of a meltdown.

"Okay, let me think about it." After a long pause, he said, "I'm going to head to the field in a few hours, but if you need anything, I can come home."

The disappointment of reality was setting in, and I wasn't ready to face it. "Do you want to quit it all, pack up, and live in a hut in Costa Rica?" It was a serious question, but he didn't take the bait.

"Oh, yeah? How will we pay our bills?" he asked with an undertone of playful sarcasm that didn't upset me.

"Well, we wouldn't have many bills because we'd leave all of this behind," I retorted.

He chimed in just as fast, and I could tell he wasn't going to go there with me even though I wanted him to. "What about our families?" he gently whispered.

"We are gone nine months of the year anyway. We could just come back and visit," I said with watery eyes.

He sat on the bed with me, realizing I just needed space to grieve and verbally process my escape plan from my life, no matter how unrealistic my suggestions were.

At that moment, I hated baseball and how it was taking my husband away from me when I needed him most. It was a lifestyle that gave us so much experientially and financially, yet it took so much more away mentally and emotionally. Moments like these reminded me of how I longed for just a single weekend to be together without worrying about my husband's travel schedule. He was leaving for a road trip in a couple of days, and I hadn't even begun to process what it would feel like to be alone with the weight of my sadness.

Silence filled the room as we both just sat in the bed, basking in the few moments we had together before he left for the field.

Fighting the silence, RR asked, "Do you want to listen to music?"

My answer was no, but I said, "Sure."

"It might be good for you," he said quietly. I know he was worried about me. He'd never seen me like that before. I had never seen myself like that before.

His comment annoyed me, but I wasn't even sure why, and I knew he was right. I would have sat in my sadness, feeling sorry for myself all day if it wasn't for him.

He opened his phone and turned on the song "You'll Come" by Hillsong.

The lyrics say:

> *As surely as the sun will rise*
> *You'll come to us*
> *Certain as the dawn appears*
> *You'll come*
> *Let Your glory fall as You respond to us*
> **Spirit rain**
> *Flood into our thirsty hearts again*[1]

Silent and holy tears poured down my face as I looked up into my husband's eyes to thank him. Tears are a baptism of the soul.

Before I could get out any words, he said, "What about Spirit Rain?" He meant as a baby name.

My heart softened, and I leaned into his chest, waiting for more tears to come, but they were all dried up. I blew my nose in his shirt—the one he was wearing to the field and nodded my head with a deep yes, still looking into his eyes and thinking that this must be what "in sickness and in health" really means.

"Spirit Rain is perfect," I said with the first ounce of peace I had felt in days.

RR left for the field. Giving our baby a name helped me hold onto a semblance of comfort, and it would remind me in the haze of the coming twelve months that my baby was real, and one day I might feel the glory of the Divine fall on me once again.

But certainly not for a while.

* * *

TWO YEARS EARLIER

"Robbie Ross's wife!" one fan yelled at me when I dropped off Robbie at the stadium in Texas. That was my new name and title.

They didn't mean anything by it; after all, I was Robbie's wife. But, even then, I shuddered a little. My subconscious rejected the idea of my entire identity being shrunk down to who I was married to. To this day, when someone calls me Robbie Ross's wife, my hope in the growth of society crumbles a little.

My whole life, I had been the black girl at a white, Christian school, and then I became Robbie Ross's wife. I went from being given one identity to another—never having defined my identity for myself or even knowing that was an option. I didn't have the language to describe it at the time, but my heart knew something was wrong with that concept. Society was shrinking me into a box.

Even so, right on cue, I smiled robotically and waved back.

Some of the more die-hard fans stood outside of the tunnel that the players entered before games. Players showed up for 7:00 p.m. games anywhere from 11:00 a.m. to 2:00 p.m. The tunnel is a private entrance for players, family, management, and George Bush—yes, the former President, who was also a part owner of the Texas Rangers—. We would drive down a long stretch of the driveway while fans lined the grassy sides of the hill leading up to the covered garage, which led to the clubhouse, family rooms, offices, and all the hidden parts of the stadium that no one got to see but us.

Fans knew the players' vehicles better than anyone. They could point out which player was in which car no matter how tinted the windows. And all of us had our windows tinted.

The fans would yell and wave in hopes that they could get the players' attention. Often, they were creative, bringing signs or dressing up. They made a thing of it, bringing their coolers for lunch, lawn chairs, and picnic blankets. Some players waved through the window, but the fans' true goal was to get the players to stop and sign autographs. Some fans were there for fun, and others were there to get their cards signed that they would later sell online.

RR was a fan favorite in Texas. When he made it to the big leagues with the Rangers, they named a helmet-sized nacho bowl after him which was called Rossome Nachos. He wore a pink backpack and rode a stick horse between his legs every day before games. It was supposed to be a one-week rookie prank, but fans loved it so much (and so did he) that the veteran players made him wear the costume the entire season. Robbie is always a good sport when it comes to getting attention.

The first time a fan called me "Robbie Ross's wife," I thought I was imagining it. But when the same fan brought a poster that said, "Robbie, say hello to Mrs. Robbie Ross for me," I realized that my husband's job was a bigger deal than I thought and that our lifestyle was far from normal.

People knew us, but we didn't know them. Which was very strange to come to terms with for this small-town girl from Kentucky. Through some sort of odd societal conditioning, I eventually knew my job was to smile and play the role. From the outside looking in, this likely sounds thrilling, but it made me want to hide. And it furthered my pursuit of perfecting and pretending. I had an image to keep up.

I was seen but not known—which made me more insecure than ever. No one knew I was struggling with crippling anxiety. I could barely get out of bed on days RR was on the road. Normal things like going to the grocery store, driving on the highway, or walking my dogs felt like exhausting, paralyzing tasks—not to mention making friends in a city I wasn't familiar with. I wrestled with the guilt of not seizing the day, and a life everyone told me was a once-in-a-lifetime opportunity. I knew it was, but my anxiety didn't care. Anxiety doesn't play by the rules.

I eventually learned to become friends with the fans. To show them we are just regular people living a not-so-regular life, which lightened the tension between being seen and being known. Social media helped with that a little. I could show people real parts of our life instead of just being written about online by others who didn't know us.

Up to this point, there was no greater pressure in my life than when my husband was at the peak of his career as a professional baseball player. RR was drafted by the Texas Rangers right out of high school in 2008. I went to college, and he went to minor league Spring Training. While I was attending class, he was climbing his way to the big leagues.

When rumors circulated around that he was going to be drafted straight out of high school, I assumed he was going to war.

Bless my heart.

Baseball people had their own language, and I did not speak it. I started to understand the magnitude of RR's talent when I noticed how the professional scouts raised their radar guns to gauge ball speed when RR was pitching but not for anyone else. I wasn't even sure what a scout or a radar gun was, but I could see that, out of all the players at our small private school, they were only interested in RR. Still, I had no idea I was in love with a man who would make a career out of playing a game.

Even though there were moments in high school when I got glimpses of his talent, I simply had no idea what it would mean to be married to a baseball player. I am not sure RR even knew all that came with the lifestyle.

Of course, there were games every night—162 regular season games, to be exact. That doesn't include Spring Training or playoffs. Baseball is not just a job or a career, it is a lifestyle, and it asks that the entire family give their everything to make it to the top. On average, his team played in six different states per month, traveling by plane overnight in the big leagues or sleeper buses in the minor leagues. As glorious as the lifestyle is (because, at times, it absolutely is!) and seems, there are also hidden horrors (because, at times, it is smoke and mirrors).

Yes, there were red carpets, VIP access to restaurants, celebrations, concerts, charity events, and big league contracts to strive for. But there was also a great deal of uncertainty and no sense of emotional, financial, or career security. One minute you can be in the big leagues, and the next, you can be released. And when I say a minute, I mean that fully. A single moment can change your entire life. If you are lucky, you find out from the management themselves. If you aren't, you find out on Twitter that your entire life has changed because the news of a trade has leaked, and someone has tweeted about it and tagged you. You pack up and move all your things across the country within forty-eight hours or less.

And for spouses, there were absurd rules taught to the newcomer "rookie wives" by veteran wives. For example, girlfriends of the players were not allowed on the family trips or at Bible study. There was also a dress code. "Shorts aren't a good representation of our husbands' brand," a veteran wife told us rookies. By "brand" she meant public image.

For those of you who are baseball fans, you might recognize a baseball wife at a game by what she's wearing. We are the only ones dressed like we aren't at a baseball game. To everyone else, this is a sporting event. To us, it's our husband's career, our second home, and according to some wives, our opportunity to represent our husband's brand. Considering mine wore a pink backpack and horse between his legs every day as part of a rookie prank, and I had no idea what I was doing. I suppose we were the perfect couple.

Baseball wives are often with other baseball wives or alone, but we know all the seat attendants, season ticket holders, and security. We can navigate the stadium better than anyone else there, even the players. We know exactly what is happening in the game by the sound of the crowd's roar or the crack of the bat without even looking at the field.

Oddly enough, I got used to the absurd rules that no one seemed to question. Being a baseball wife was overwhelmingly similar to being a part of Country Club Christianity. Even though I knew the system players' wives lived by was entitled and catty at best, who was I to question it? I was one of them now, at least in name.

But somewhere inside, I knew I'd never fit in. To put things simply, I was just not put together enough. My big messy curls matched my big messy heart. I was allergic to small talk, which was not a popular allergy in some baseball wife circles. And I was always accidentally breaking their unwritten rules, making me loved by some (for being oblivious) or hated by a few (for not respecting their faux authority). I was embarrassing myself as I tried to figure out my place as a baseball wife and learn how to be a wife, woman, and adult married to someone who placed me in the spotlight. It was a tiny spotlight compared to RR's, but it was enough to make me want to hide.

Eventually, I found my way, but it would take things like public humiliation to remind me that, while I am just a normal girl from Kentucky, I did not live a normal life.

A fan tweeted a picture of me eating a popsicle in the stands, which sounds harmless. But that single photo rocked my world: "Robbie Ross' wife deep-throating a popsicle. What I would do to be that popsicle."

It wasn't the most clever or original caption, but the amount of attention someone paid to my eating a popsicle was uncomfortably invasive, to say the least. I learned that you never knew when people were watching, so it's best to pretend as if they always are. Not to mention, the picture itself was mortifying. You know when your popsicle is melting, so you attempt not to drip on yourself by sticking more of the popsicle in your mouth? Yeah. Well. You can imagine.

I read it during the game and sank into my chair like quicksand. I went into a daze as I thought about being surrounded by 50,000 people inside the stadium with no escape plan.

It was over ninety degrees that day with a heat index of 102. Texans were counting the consecutive days that held a record heat index that summer, like living on the sun's surface was something to brag about. If you aren't familiar with Texas heat, just imagine walking around with a blow dryer on high heat blowing in your face and all over your body for four straight months.

Unfortunately, I was not dressed for the occasion. My light gray maxi dress was not even close to being sweatproof. Squirming in my chair, where I had just been caught going ham on the popsicle, I realized there was no escape: I was surely sweating through my dress. Anxiety sweat just hits differently, ya know? Reading that tweet and seeing my profile with a bomb pop halfway down my throat made it clearer that I did not have my shit together.

My time as a WAG (Wives and Girlfriends of Athletes) with the Texas Rangers was equivalent to my freshman year of high school. I was not purposefully standing out; I just was. It did not help that I wasn't what people expected, as I'd often been told since we started dating when I was fourteen years old.

I get it. A small-town baseball player who wears camo, was born and bred on a farm, and shows up to the big leagues with a biracial wife. She wears "hippie clothes," shows up late to the games, and doesn't abide by any rules because she lives in her head. Nothing about me was what people expected. But I had to remind myself that this was why RR chose me.

Sophomore year of high school, RR, my boyfriend of a solid three weeks, of a solid three weeks, caught me gossiping to a friend about other girls.

Without hesitating, he confronted me, "I wanted to date you because you weren't a drama girl. So, are you a drama girl or not?"

"No, I'm not in drama," I responded, trying to deflect the question with humor.

"Then why are you gossiping about the other girls? Who cares what they're doing?" he said.

He was right. I walked away feeling both the embarrassment of being called out and the attraction to a boy that would later become my husband for calling me to become someone better.

He saw me, the real me, and he asked me to behave like her, not like the other girls. I was in love with RR because he loved me in a way that helped me love myself. He reminded me of who I was before the world told me who I was. And isn't that what love does best? If it isn't calling us to become someone more like Jesus, then is it really love at all?

* * *

We spent three seasons with the Texas Rangers before RR was traded to the Boston Red Sox. I made some of my best friends being a Texas Rangers baseball wife. But when we moved to Boston, I was thankful to have made it out alive.

Once we got there, I realized I needed to find myself apart from my public role. This was around the time my Gran died, before I found out I was pregnant. I was questioning my life's purpose. Could it really be to go to baseball games every night and cheer on my husband as he pursued his dream while I had none of my own?

These thoughts are perhaps why I started something completely new: yoga teacher training.

On my first day of Yoga Teacher Training (YTT), in a big room with wooden floors and the smell of incense surrounding all twelve of the newest Health Yoga Life teacher trainees, the teachers skipped the small talk and went straight for the soul. I knew I was in the right place. I didn't know it yet, but by moving, breathing, and meditating on my yoga mat, I was about to learn how a person can lose their religion and yet find faith.

Three sisters led our eight-week program to become certified yoga instructors. But more than that, they were our guides back home to ourselves—home to our wild and free hearts, where it was possible to live in alignment with our souls. Yoga became my therapy—along with my actual therapist.

"Who are you?" Ida, one of the sisters leading YTT, asked us. Twelve perfect strangers sat in a circle staring awkwardly but intentionally at each other.

Erin went first. She was the only mom in the group, and her confidence roared. She wore no makeup and had short brown hair. She spoke three languages, ran businesses, and had a husband and children at home. She spoke with humility, explaining why she signed up for YTT. "I am a wife. Mother. Chef. Translator. I am here to rediscover myself after having kids."

I couldn't believe she had the confidence to admit she was here for that reason. I mean, I was too. But I couldn't even admit it to myself, let alone a room full of women I barely knew.

Who the hell am I? I thought to myself. *How am I going to come up with anything impressive?* I was still reaching for my trusty frenemy, perfectionism.

All twelve people in the circle gave their names, roles, and titles like they were interviewing for a job. It was like they had practiced this before—they came prepared for the assignment. But I—a basic nomad with no real title to boast about—sat in discomfort as the others shared their impressive lists. We were in Boston, after all, home of some of the best schools, hospitals, and research centers in the world. I was thankful to be the last in the circle to answer. Brand-new to Boston, with not a friend in sight, it was my turn to answer the question, "Who are you?"

"My name is Brittany Ross. I am a baseball wife. I am basically the CEO of mine and my husband's life. And I am not even really sure what that means or why I am here. Nice to meet you all." That's it. That's the best I could come up with. I didn't have a job title to impress them with. I didn't know why I'd come here. But I smiled, knowing at least I was honest.

Did I want to become a yoga teacher? I didn't know. Did I have time to be a yoga teacher considering my travel schedule and the pace of my life? Probably not. Who hires a yoga teacher that only lives in one place for less than six months?

Before the embarrassment of my pitiful answer could set in, Ida, the head yoga teacher, commanded the room. She was thin but strong. She smiled when she spoke and walked lightly on her feet. She seemed to float. She addressed the room: "Okay. Who are you without all your roles and titles? Before you got a job, had a baby, got married, even before you had a name, you were a soul. Who is that soul?"

Well, frick. I pressed my lips together, fully expecting to go first this time around. It took everything in me to come up with the term "baseball wife." I was just going to have to be honest again. Tears welled up in my eyes, and I blinked them away. I was surprised by how emotional I was letting myself get in front of strangers.

Ida spoke again, "This time, instead of saying who we were out loud to the group, we will write it down in our journals. Come back to this page at the end of teacher training, so you can reflect."

Thank you, Jesus. I closed my eyes and took a deep breath, thankful not to have to admit the truth out loud to my new Bostonian friends.

"I don't know who I am," I wrote it down in my blank journal. The words seemed bolder as I looked at them, wondering what else I should write. I scribbled on my paper and pretended to be writing, shoving down my thoughts of inadequacy, anxiously waiting for everything to be over.

Mere seconds before our writing time was over, I wrote: "At least I am being honest. Maybe that's a start." Then, I closed my journal, never wanting to acknowledge that truth again.

Ida said, "Before you were born, you were a soul. That soul has a purpose. Yoga Teacher Training will teach you how to become a yoga teacher, but it will also point you in the direction of your life's purpose. It will show you who you are beyond your roles and titles. And hopefully, the practice will lead you back to hope. Back to trust. Back to love. Back to yourself."

As terrified as I was, I knew I was in the right place. For the first time in a long time, I felt like I could breathe again. Those words and everything that showed up in my heart while I was on my yoga mat would get me through what came next.

chapter six

MISCARRIAGE

I WANTED TO BE GOOD. I just didn't know good would never be good enough.

It was finally the off-season. RR and I were back home in Kentucky after a long drive home from Boston and a disappointing 2015 baseball season. We finished last in our division and did not make it to the playoffs like the Red Sox usually did. As disappointing as baseball season was, I was ready to be in my own home and focus on having a baby. The pace of my lifestyle was catching up to me, and rest was calling my name.

We pulled up to the farm and the crisp fall Kentucky air felt like a friendly hug. It was October, the best month of the year. Our anniversary month. We would be celebrating in just a couple of weeks.

I brought my frozen mason jar home in a cooler with ice packs like I was carrying an organ for a transplant. We took the frozen mason jar to RR's parents' farm and buried our baby on their property. It was a final goodbye to my first baby and a step into the unknown of what a miscarriage said about my body. I entered an unwelcome stage of grief called acceptance.

RR pointed to a spot in the middle of a field that you could see from his parent's back porch and said, "That looks like a good spot."

He was used to burying things on the farm. Growing up in the country made him more accustomed to death than I was. Death, funerals, and goodbyes made me queasy and uncomfortable in my skin. But this death was different, heavier.

He grabbed a shovel from the barn and led the way as the farm dog, Duke, followed us while sniffing the mason jar. We were both quiet but at peace, even though we understood the gravity of what we were doing. Months had passed since I miscarried, and the numbness of grief had set in.

RR started digging a hole, and I sat down with Duke letting the sun hit me in the face. *The sun heals*, I thought. I crossed my legs and put my hands on my knees, taking some intentional breaths as I watched him shovel more dirt from the ground to bury our baby. Grief is wild in this way: it anchors you to the present like no other feeling. My breath felt like the only thing I could control. And it was.

"Did you ever think you'd be doing this?" I asked.

"No, never." He replied. "Life is crazy," he continued.

Duke nestled into my lap and rolled over for a tummy scratch. My in-laws' farm is 34 acres, so we had a special and private moment while my father-in-law was at work and my mother-in-law sat in her office inside the house where RR grew up.

"Okay, it's ready." RR said. He stood for a moment in the sun with the shovel still in his hands. "Do you want to put it in there?"

"No, will you do it?" RR was always brave for me when I didn't have the strength.

I couldn't find the words, so I said nothing else.

RR prayed and covered the hole with dirt, and we both said, "Goodbye, Spirit Rain. We will see you in heaven one day."

For me, there were two parts to the grief of having a miscarriage. The grief of losing a baby is an actual loss that only a mother who's lost her child can understand. The guilt of what I could have done differently. The worry of if the baby felt any pain or abandonment by me, their mother. And the grief of losing the pregnancy. What could have been but was no more. Letting go of the idea of being pregnant simultaneously with my other pregnant friends and planning the nursery, buying clothes, finding out the gender, and sharing those cute ultrasound pictures online with friends and family.

My in-laws' farm is now an organic flower farm that grows beautiful blooms for our local Whole Foods as well as for weddings and Mother's Day gifts. Those flowers reminded me that beautiful things come out of dust. God brings beauty from ashes.

On the car ride home, RR turned to me and said, "Do you ever think about eternity?"

"I do. All the time. Sometimes I wonder why God doesn't just end all of this and let us live forever in heaven. With no pain, no suffering. The way we were supposed to," I said confidently.

"But doesn't it freak you out? Like forever is a long time—it never ends."

"I know. This might sound weird, but I can't wait for forever. To be with Gran and our baby—all of us together."

He slowed down at the stop sign before the turn onto the main road and grabbed his head with both hands like he always does when we talk about eternity. He rubbed his eyes with the palms of his hands and moved them back and forth like he was trying to snap himself out of a bad dream.

"I just can't even think about it," he said anxiously. RR does okay with death, but the thought of what happens after totally freaks him out.

It had been a while since we talked about eternity, but I was used to how he felt about it. RR has a calm, cool, and collected attitude about most serious things in life, but he has a deeply held fear about the unknowns of eternity. Thinking about it is the only time anything serious works him up. Ever since my Gran died, though, I love to think about eternity. It is the only thing that makes sense to me when I think about God– that there would be a place where our souls reside forever without a single bit of suffering. All too often, as a highly sensitive soul, I have had a deep sense that this earth is not my forever home.

But something about the thought of eternity really shook RR up. That is how I felt about death. Death feels so unnatural to me that I can't comprehend it. Like a glitch in the system of life.

We both agreed to move to the next subject, knowing we had been down that rabbit hole before. I reached over and squeezed his hand, and we rode silently the rest of the way home.

* * *

I had found a rhythm of grief, even though life was moving on, and I didn't want it to. That is one of those sneaky ways grief can come up behind you and stop you in your tracks. As you sit there, a gaping hole in your heart and your life made by the person (or people, in my case) you lost, the world just keeps moving on as if nothing happened. The globe doesn't stop turning; life doesn't stop moving; the sun doesn't stop rising or setting— nothing stops even though your life has been rocked to the core. That reality is both deeply offensive and unspeakably comforting. The fact that even our darkest days are not strong enough to stop the orchestration of the universe reminds me someone far bigger than I can comprehend is holding it all together—even when I cannot.

The propensity of society to keep moving forward, heal from (or repress) your loss, and move on almost makes it feel like having to say goodbye to that person once again. Because, even though the loss hurts, when you're in the thick of those days of grief, the feelings and emotions are so strong and overwhelming that they almost serve as a way to keep you connected to your lost loved one. And when life moves away from that, it can feel like moving away from the ones you lost, too.

But through it all, I had my eyes set on getting pregnant again, and I counted down the months, weeks, and days until we could try to get pregnant again. Perhaps, it was a method of distracting myself from this horrible season of loss. According to my doctor, I needed to wait three months before we started trying again. *Trying* to get pregnant was so unfamiliar to me. *Trying* meant tracking ovulation and planning sex around when a white stick with a blue cap showed me my fertile window with a digital smiley face.

The Academy, the private Christian school I attended from first grade through high school graduation, taught us a few things about sex: that sex led to pregnancy, and pregnancy and sex before marriage were bad. Therefore, don't have sex until you are married. Remaining sexually pure was the ultimate testament of faith, and there was even a blip in time when all my friends got purity rings from their fathers to mark their purity. I didn't have a father around, and I didn't receive a ring.

And we were taught that when you are married and having sex, you will have a baby. But that wasn't the entire picture, and it skewed reality for many girls who grew up with the teachings of purity culture.

In Linda Kay Klein's book, *Pure,* she describes purity culture this way:

> The white, American, Evangelical Christian Purity Movement that puts emphasis on the idea that everyone is expected to maintain absolute sexlessness before marriage (that means no sexual thoughts, feelings, or actions). And upon marriage, they are expected to flip their sexuality on like a light switch. Men are taught their minds are evil, whereas women are taught their bodies are evil. Purity culture also teaches

that women are responsible for the sexual thoughts, feelings and choices men make, and so must dress, walk and talk in just the right way so as not to "inspire" sexual thoughts, feelings, and actions in them. If they do "inspire" such thoughts, they are said to be a "stumbling block" – literally a thing over which men trip on their pathway to God.[2]

In purity culture teachings, it is not uncommon to hear the examples of a classroom full of students being asked to unwrap a lollipop and lick it, passing it to the person next to them to lick it too. There may have been a few brave people who actually licked the lollipop following their classmate. The teacher would make the example, pointing out that by the time the lollipop got passed around a few times, no one would want that lollipop anymore. And then make the comparison to that of a girl who has sex before she is married. The emphasis on having sex to make a baby (which is the ultimate goal of a good southern woman) only adds to the pressure for women (and men) who have obeyed all the rules of purity culture and still come face to face with miscarriage and fertility struggles.

Purity culture ruined a generation of women I was a part of by shaming young girls into believing our bodies were bad. Our bodies were seen as a temptation for the boys that couldn't keep their thoughts out of the gutter and ultimately taught girls that boys couldn't think with their brains but only with their balls.

And this ultimately led to us not understanding our own bodies at all. I hadn't thought about the teachings of purity culture in years, but it had somehow leaked into my five-year marriage as a grown-ass woman. I realized how little I knew about sex, making a baby, and my own female body. No twenty-five-year-old woman should be actively trying to conceive at the same time she learns that there is only a certain window of time throughout a month in which she can conceive a child.

Regardless of how little I knew, and even though I deeply rejected the idea that a woman finds her worth in the title of motherhood, it did not stop my desire to become one from growing. There is a unique ferocity inside of a woman who has her heart set on motherhood. Ask any woman who has experienced a miscarriage or held a negative test in one hand and sobbed into the other month after month of being told yet again she is not pregnant.

And for the love of God—don't ask. Stop asking. Let's normalize never asking women about their uteruses—unless you are her close friend or midwife. Trust me when I tell you that my story is one of many. Women are miscarrying at alarming rates and are given no real answers or getting to the root cause.

Regardless of how excruciating it felt to wait three months, I did as my doctor suggested in hopes that would set us up for success.

While I was waiting to try to get pregnant again, the same organization that took me to Uganda with the other Red Sox wives invited RR and I to India. When we were in Uganda, we learned that the village we were visiting had been targeted by human trafficking. Before this, I had never heard about human trafficking. Unlike today, where everyone has at least heard of human trafficking—especially thanks to the ever-popular and disturbing Ghislaine Maxwell case—prior to 2015, the average person did not know much about the darkest industry in the world.

India has one of the largest numbers of human trafficking victims. America is one of the largest contributors of human trafficking. I was passionate about empowering impoverished companies, especially women, through education. But that trip to Uganda showed me something I could never unsee.

Poor communities were being targeted for human trafficking. Due to a lack of education, resources, and options, girls were separated from their families and eventually trafficked, never to be seen by their loved ones again. There is no simple solution to ending or stopping human trafficking, but across the board, most agree that education is a crucial piece in empowering girls and women.

Still, the invitation to India made me anxious. I carried a confusing yet heavy guilt from traveling to Uganda while pregnant and ultimately losing my first baby. I reached for every reason to explain and rationalize my miscarriage to myself.

Was it the massage I got on a road trip to New York?

Was my bath water too hot?

Was there bacteria in my sandwich meat?

No guilt rang louder in my heart than blaming myself for traveling abroad in early pregnancy. Another wife on the team found out she was pregnant at the same time as me and decided not to go. Even though there was no indication that could be the reason I miscarried, I blamed myself. Pregnant women travel all the time. And women have babies in Uganda too. I still secretly blamed my on-the-go lifestyle for the reason behind my loss.

Fear made me feel like I had to decide between focusing on becoming a mother or continue traveling, but the Spirit within me stirred, and ultimately, I knew I needed to go. The Divine had something for me there. What it was, I wasn't sure. But I wanted to find out. Fear could have held me back, but all along, glimpses of my rebel spirit shone through.

Following my gut and going to India didn't mean I wasn't scared. But the prompting was so strong for me to go that I felt like I would be directly denying a conviction if I didn't.

Little drops of divinity like that were offered to me along the journey. But when I look back and ask myself why I chose to do the brave thing and travel abroad despite my fears and worries, it's because deep down, I wanted to find the faith I saw in people like Tony. I knew there was no way to find what I was looking for by sitting on the couch at home.

Good Christian girls, after all, don't always travel into the unknown. They often choose the safe and mundane option. I wanted to break free from that mold and follow the Divine into the wild rebellion against the idea that to be good and Christian, women must live up to their ultimate calling of being a mom. I wanted both. And I knew I'd be disappointed in myself if I didn't go and do the brave thing.

If I couldn't ever become a mother, then at least I was displaying bravery in this area. And if I did by some miracle become one, what kind of woman did I want to be for my children? One who let fear be the boss of her? Or one who chose to believe God is for us, not against us, even when it seems like all hope is lost?

On a spiritual level, I can't help but look back and see that I was invited into the darkest industry in the world by the Divine while walking through the darkest season of my own life. Had that invitation come at any other time, I would have never met Renu, Mission 108 would not exist, and without a doubt, I would have never begun walking in alignment with my soul.

And that is how I ended up in India in the first place. One yes to Uganda led to an invitation to India that I couldn't turn down, led to a yes to partnering with a safe home program that was rescuing girls out of sex trafficking, which led to a commitment to always look for hope where things seem hopeless.

One thing I have learned is that to find the light, we must first face the darkness.

* * *

I found out I was pregnant for the second time right after my first trip to India. I had suspected I was pregnant there but wasn't brave enough to take the test after having been pregnant the first time in Uganda. I waited three months, just like the doctor ordered, and got pregnant right after trying. Getting pregnant was not my problem—sustaining a pregnancy was.

This pregnancy and miscarriage was quicker than the first. At six weeks pregnant, I started to bleed again.

Everything started the same way: waking in the morning with cramps, blood following. The cramping intensified but never to the point of losing my breath like before. I crawled into my bed with a heating pad and was thankful that this time I was at least at home in the comfort of my own bed.

It was mid-January, and it had snowed just a couple of days before. The once perfectly white snow had turned to that ugly dark gray sludge pushed up into mounds on the side of roads. The grayness of the day reflected the state of my heart. RR insisted we go to the hospital. Even though I knew there was nothing they could do, it felt like the thing I was *supposed* to do. My father-in-law met us there, hoping that he could intercede with prayer.

I knew what was happening. If hope could have saved this baby, it would have. We sat in the hospital's waiting room with a completely different care team than before since we were back home in Kentucky. Not only was the team different, but so was the care. The doctor and nurse acted as if this was a normal, natural occurrence and didn't seem remotely affected by my loss. Losing a baby at six weeks felt no less than losing one at ten.

The ultrasound confirmed the loss, and I was told to come back in a week to make sure my HCG levels were falling like they were supposed to. So, I went home to miscarry in my bed.

We named our second miscarried baby Sage. Sage means wisdom and is a tribute to my Native American ancestors. Americans know sage for its most common western use: smudging. Smudging is a ceremony for purifying or cleansing the soul of negative thoughts or space of negative energy. And Sage was my Gran's favorite spice.

Grief, on top of grief, weighs on the spirit—and the grief just kept piling on. The advice from my doctor to wait three months wasn't the recipe for a healthy and successful pregnancy like I thought it would be.

With my eyes set on motherhood with an even greater desire than before, in mid-February, right before we left for Spring Training, I took another pregnancy test.

PREGNANT.

Three pregnancies in less than a year. My hope was the third time's a charm.

chapter seven

UNPACKING

EASTER WEEKEND CAME TEN WEEKS later. The off-season had flown by. RR and I were back in Spring Training in Fort Myers, Florida. I found a doctor through some of the other baseball wives, who were used to being passed around from doctor to doctor for their pregnancies during baseball season. Pregnancy is longer than baseball season, so we often have a doctor in each city we live in.

At my ten-week appointment, the doctor squeezed cold gel on my stomach for the external ultrasound so I could see my baby. Doctor Bell was enthusiastic about this pregnancy, and I loved the energy he brought to the room. I was ten-plus weeks along, and I had never been pregnant longer than this.

Third time's a charm? I told myself with nervous energy.

Right there on the screen, I could see my little tadpole-sized baby. I'd become familiar enough with ultrasounds to know what to look for. Right as she found the perfect spot on my belly, we saw my baby's perfect little heartbeat.

I smiled and thanked God quietly.

Squeezing RR's hand and feeling the anxious sweat roll from my armpits down my sides. We looked at each other, not quite knowing what to say. RR has a particular grin he wears when he feels excited but nervous. His ears move upward a little, and those endearing perfect lines we call crow's feet jet out of the creases of his eyes when he genuinely grins. I hadn't seen that grin in a long time but didn't realize it until now.

For a moment, while still holding his hand, I thought about the grief he must have been experiencing and silently holding onto. He said the words "I'm fine" often, but at this this moment of relief, his shoulders shrugged down, his breath returned to normal, and his face expressed joy which told me he hadn't been fine. He, too, had been hiding his emotions from the world, me, and from himself.

The truth of the day was that I was pregnant with a healthy baby. Even though one thousand other fears tried to crowd into my heart, I had to cling onto the truth of that day, that moment really. Anxiety had the power to ruin it all for me. I knew stress would do nothing but rob me of the joy of the current truth that I was pregnant with a healthy baby.

* * *

The full truth was that seeing a heartbeat didn't mean much for my pregnancies. It didn't guarantee a healthy baby, pregnancy, or anything in between. But it was something.

The ultrasound tech took some measurements, typed some things in the computer, and told me that I was likely ten weeks pregnant.

"You will come back for another ultrasound next week," she said as I rolled my high-waisted leggings back to cover my belly since the ultrasound was complete. "We will look at the baby next week and make sure everything looks alright. Since we don't have a last period to go off of for you, we'll just make sure the baby is growing on track."

RR and I walked to the car with ultrasound pictures in hand, feeling both excited for good news and anxious about being ten weeks pregnant—exactly where I was when I lost my first baby.

"I just need to get to twelve weeks. The chances of miscarrying in your second trimester go way down," I told RR as we drove back to our Spring Training rental.

The following week, we headed to our doctor's appointment with more hope than we'd felt in months. I went through my usual routine of waiting in the lobby with all the other expectant mothers, admiring their bellies and hoping that one day I would be in their shoes. I stood up as I heard my name called and navigated back to the room after checking my weight and blood pressure. I rolled my leggings past my belly button and took a few deep breaths.

There's a distinct and cold kind of emptiness inside the womb of a woman having a miscarriage. A baby with a loud heartbeat, like a trotting horse, is supposed to fill that space. And when it doesn't, you feel the emptiness not only inside your womb but also inside your heart.

The ultrasound tech was different that week, so I felt like I had to explain my history to her. "I've had two back-to-back miscarriages over the last year. Last week we saw the heartbeat. This week we are hoping to hear it and make sure the baby is growing okay. I am eleven weeks."

She continued taking the measurements. Her body language didn't change, and I couldn't read her. She was stoic, possibly bored or over-worked, but certainly unphased by the information I had just offered. She seemed to be moving quicker with the ultrasound than the time I was here before. But maybe I was reading into it. Or maybe this was a good thing.

She left the room and said, "Dr. Bell will be with you shortly."

RR and I looked at each other and took a collective deep breath as we heard a knock. Before we responded, the door swung open.

Doctor Bell walked in with a melancholy energy, but his face was still cheerful. I studied his body language from the moment he entered the room. He sat down on his stool and clasped his hands together.

"The baby has shrunk in size since our last appointment." Dr. Bell said, looking directly into my eyes.

My eyes widened, and I could feel my heartbeat in my ears. I took a deep breath waiting for him to say more. I was used to this, but it still wasn't easy.

"Okay." I said, pursing my lips together. I wanted to cry but nothing came. I was numb.

"Usually when we see a baby has shrunk in size, it's the beginning stages of a miscarriage or a missed miscarriage," Doctor Bell said.

I shook my head and glanced back at the ultrasound screen, which was now dark black. Just like my uterus.

"What is a missed miscarriage?" I asked, defeated. Without allowing him to answer, I moved on to my next question.

"Could the progesterone I am taking have anything to do with this?" I had been using hormonal progesterone suppositories in hopes of sustaining this pregnancy.

Doctor Bell went on to tell me how progesterone worked. Everything from there on out was a blur; I checked out of my body like I often did out of self-preservation and felt my blood turn cold. Nothing he said mattered.

* * *

I had surpassed sadness. Back in the car with my face buried in my hands, I went straight to anger. "How is this happening to me, Robbie?" None of this was making sense.

"I don't know, Britt. I'm so sorry, buddy."

"Why do bad things happen to good people?" I demanded. I directed my anger at him, but he knew I wasn't actually upset with him. I let it all spill out without giving RR any time to respond.

"This isn't fair! Why is my body abandoning me? Why is God abandoning me? Abandoning us? Am I really this unfit to be a mother?" Slamming my fists onto my legs.

It was Easter weekend. I didn't want anything to do with God, let alone His promises. I was living my own version of Good Friday and Holy Saturday. We can only call them good and Holy because we know Sunday came.

But that wasn't the case for me. There seemed nothing good or holy about this.

Two weeks passed, and I still had not started the miscarriage process. I guess this is what Dr. Bell meant by missed miscarriage. A missed miscarriage is when a baby has died in the womb, but the mother hasn't had any symptoms, such as bleeding or pain. The body has not recognized the loss, and the symptoms of miscarriage don't begin on their own.

Carrying death inside of my body but still going about my life as normal was the peak of my anxiety. Every time I went to the bathroom in a public place, I held my breath, hoping there wasn't any blood. All my pregnancy symptoms were gone. It was just a matter of time.

Spring Training was coming to an end, which meant it was time for RR to fly out to another city with the team for opening day. And I was going to drive twenty-three hours from Florida to Boston, hoping and wishing on a prayer that I did not start the miscarriage process while I was on the road in a random city.

What will I do if this happens while I am driving?

My anxiety had never been so intense. And the only ease for my anxiety was to mentally escape my body and avoid thinking about my reality. I busied myself with packing and focused on getting to the next destination. I had a full day's worth of driving to think about all of this. Three miscarriages. Something had to be wrong.

What was I going to do next?

With nothing but time to think, I determined that I could trace back most of the loss of my identity and purpose to shame. The feeling of enoughness. I wasn't black enough. I wasn't white enough. I wasn't a good enough wife. I wasn't a good enough Christian. And now I wasn't good enough to become a mother.

Who is even writing the script that begets our belonging? Who decides if we are enough or not? Was it society, the church, or the circles I ran in? Or was it me? And why was I subscribing to that narrative in the first place?

If you had looked at my Instagram, you would see a life of wonder, travel, excitement, and fun. And all of that was real and true. But under all of that, I was dying on the inside. My insides did not match my outside, and I wanted that to change, no matter the cost. I knew I couldn't keep chasing perfectionism and pretending while my soul shrunk.

Growing up, I was the welcomed outlier. The black sheep of sorts. Born a little extra sensitive, so I walked through life with an extra dose of anxiety. I always sensed that this world was not my home but ultimately realized I had to figure out how to live here anyway. I suppose I chose perfectionism as a coping mechanism to survive a life where I didn't belong.

Survival. That thought led me back to a moment with Renu and the girls at the safe house. When it started to get dark, the girls and staff would build a fire. One night while we were there, RR started to take the lead on building the fire by asking for a lighter. The girls all gathered around and laughed at his question.

Renu stepped in and grabbed the sticks from his hands, laughing and slightly annoyed that he would overstep on her job. I grinned and felt proud that she was confident enough to take back her power from a man. It was her job to start the fire. The right and responsibility were hers. You could see the fire burning in her eyes after years of being trampled over by men.

Renu bent down and rubbed her twigs together. Within seconds, a spark lit and the fire grew. I watched in amazement as I realized how little I knew about survival. But the girls knew. They were no longer victims of human trafficking; they were survivors. A thought rolled through my mind, and I tried to shove it down out of guilt: *I want to be like them. Like Renu.*

They had been through so much. It felt rude to even think such a thing. But it wasn't their external circumstances that I envied. It was their internal strength, resilience, and the joy they exuded despite what they had been through. They had fought for joy and won. I wanted that victory too.

I couldn't relate to not knowing where my next meal would come from or being coerced into trafficking. I would never know the depth of their pain. But one thing both the girls in the safe home and I could relate to was we were both fighting for the same things: to overcome fear, find healing, and become free.

* * *

I made the full twenty-three-hour drive from Florida to Boston without starting the miscarriage. *Relief.* When I walked through the door to our new rental house in Boston, our mattress was on the floor, and our entire house was packed in boxes. This was usually a good distraction—making a house somewhat of a home for the six months of baseball season was my specialty. Since we traveled a total of nine months of the year (two months for Spring Training, six months for regular season baseball, and one month of playoffs), I always knew how to make our rental houses feel more like home. Although nothing felt comforting when I was losing my baby.

There was an unexpected snowstorm in Boston at the beginning of April. Snowstorms in Boston are not a light dusting of snow like they are back home in Kentucky. They were flight-canceling and have-to-wait-two-days to travel kind of storms. RR was starting the season in Toronto, Canada, just a short flight away from Boston—but not in the middle of a storm. He insisted he would come home to be with me once I started bleeding. But I was so sick of my own sadness, I didn't want anyone else to take part in it anymore. I wanted to do this one alone.

A few days passed, and I had barely unpacked anything but clothes. There were no signs of a miscarriage starting. I curled up on my mattress with a few towels I found in a mislabeled box. Using the towels as blankets, I sipped on red raspberry leaf tea. Raspberry leaf is an herb used in pregnancy to tone the uterus, usually in the third trimester, to encourage contractions. I used it to encourage my uterus to start contracting because of the missed miscarriage.

Just a few hours later, I started cramping and the miscarriage began. I drew a bath for myself and tried to make myself as comfortable as possible, knowing fully what to expect. As I laid in the bathtub of my rental house in Boston, I verbally coached myself through my third miscarriage.

This is the last time I will ever do this.

You never have to do this again.

This has all been too much.

It is time I start taking care of myself.

I am never trying to get pregnant again.

You can do this.

You can do this.

You can do this.

Breathe.

I told myself nothing would ever be the same after this. I wasn't just losing my baby, I was shedding all the layers of this person I had become but didn't recognize. A woman finds out who she is when she meets herself in her darkest hours.

Who am I?

I thought back to Yoga Teacher Training and still didn't know the answer.

The soothing, warm bathwater made it easier to get through the waves of increasing pain. There was something liberating about being alone and having no eyes on me. There was no pressure to perform or care for others' emotional needs. I could be fully myself, yelling and moaning and breathing. For the first time in a long time, I fully let myself just be. Whatever feelings came, whether shame or guilt or sadness or anger, I let wash over me without attaching too much judgment to them. I simply let myself feel.

* * *

I knew I had two choices in those extremely tender and painful moments of miscarrying my third baby. I could either let it break me or allow it to break me open. We often only see the first choice when we are in deep pain. We think that this hard thing will break us, even kill us. There seems to be no way out, and often there isn't. But a soft whisper comes after the first option and offers us a gift. The gift is that after we feel completely broken, we realize we've just broken open. A chance to become something new.

What if around the corner from all this God-forsaken pain is an invitation? An invitation to leave behind the boxes we no longer fit inside and begin again? Maybe suffering is the birthplace of healing. Maybe I can start living in alignment with my soul. Thoughts that weren't mine but came from some deep internal knowing filled my mind and heart.

I sat up in the bath and looked across the bathroom in the mirror. I could see myself. And for the first time in a long time, I really looked at myself. Naked and staring myself in the eyes, not looking away even when I wanted to. The bags under my eyes caught my attention. I recognized those bags. I slept, but I was always tired. My soul did not know rest.

I was not just aware of Country Club Christianity. I was one of them. Pretending and perfecting my way through life but having no real connection to myself, my soul, or the Divine. Pretending is too much work for the hurting. Heartbroken people are fully vulnerable, and therefore they are the only people I can trust. Maybe I could begin to trust myself again.

I submerged myself into the water as the uterine contractions started to intensify. The once-clear bath water turned from clear to pink to red.

The water seemed to calm my uterine contractions, but the urge to push overcame me. I gripped the sides of the tub and lifted myself up to lean away from the pain. Bearing down, I pushed out my gestational sac and placenta and immediately felt relief. This time there was no mason jar to catch the remnants of my pregnancy. I was there in the water, surrounded by it all.

The physical relief that followed allowed me to stand back up in the tub. Shocked by how red the water was and, for a moment, worried about how dangerous blood loss can be during a miscarriage. Knowing no one was there in Boston to rescue me if I needed it, I drained the water and said goodbye to my baby. Once I was in the shower, and the water cleansed my skin, I closed my eyes and thought about the religion of my youth.

I cried out, screaming at God. "Why, God? Why? What have I done to deserve this?"

Country Club Christianity wasn't working out for me anymore. It felt like a bomb had gone off in my life. With each miscarriage, I found new ways to question myself and God. There was no room for perfection anymore. In fact, I wasn't even sure what box to check for religion at all. And maybe that's the point. There simply are no boxes when it comes to the Divine.

If you look at any story that involves an explosion, you will, at some point, see utter chaos. I was right in the middle of the chaos. But right after the wreckage, a change occurs. Life shifts. It becomes brilliant and bright and full of healing and hope and becoming. Perhaps, striving for "good Christian girl" was never meant for me—maybe I was always meant to be wild and free.

chapter eight

THE CURSE OF A SOUTHERN WOMAN

ALMOST A YEAR LATER, time began to take on a new meaning. Each day, my eggs were getting older, my biological clock was ticking, and I was not pregnant. My third miscarriage led to testing, labs and blood draws, procedures, and being shuffled from doctor's office to doctor's office, begging for answers and getting none. Even though we were still trying to get pregnant, I no longer seemed to be able to get pregnant at all. My body was spent.

I was numb.

Not only was I stuck in an incomprehensible loop of depression, but I was also completely consumed with becoming a mother and always looking for some new trick to try or supplement to take to fix my brokenness. I was fooling myself to think I could outrun all the pain and struggle with forced smiles, unanswered prayers, and an unhealthy dose of desiring to perfect everything around me.

My relationships eventually started to struggle as I wasn't predictable anymore. I had managed to go off and hurt many of the people I loved. Anger consumed me when people asked me when I would start having children. I would tell them bluntly that I had just miscarried and leave the energy in the room awkward and uncomfortable. When acquaintances offered unsolicited advice, I'd turn malicious and apathetic to their words. When it all felt like too much, I was done with people pleasing. I could no longer pretend to be this sweet, happy-go-lucky baseball player's wife. I was cold. Removed. Touchy.

In a way, allowing myself to process the anger and be real for once felt freeing, but in even more ways, I hated who I was becoming. I wanted to be real, but I didn't want to be angry forever. I just couldn't seem to exit the loops of anger, sadness, and grief.

The lack of control over my circumstances sent me over the edge, past the point of sanity. I'd wake up every morning rage-cleaning the house for hours, forgetting to eat or drink until 2 p.m., when my body would quite literally start shutting down. RR would leave for the field around that time, and the deep dark depression would set in. That's when I would crawl into my bed for hours and eat junk food while binge-watching trash TV.

Gametime would roll around at 7 p.m., and I would work up enough energy to put on nice clothes, and makeup and will myself out the door to go to the game and pretend like I wasn't suffering. Things were worse when RR was on the road, and I wasn't traveling to meet him. I couldn't see a reason to get out of bed at all.

I was miserable. On many levels, I knew I was not okay. But it wasn't necessarily the world I was trying to fool, it was myself.

How can this possibly be my life?

I grew weary of anyone who tried to get too close to me in fear of having to be vulnerable and totally losing my shit. If one thread was pulled in the weaving of my life, I would have completely come undone. For a person who has spent her whole life running from her emotions, only to have all of them cave in on her at once—being vulnerable is a nightmare. Being vulnerable would mean purposefully exposing my humanity and risking isolation, rejection, and judgment that I had tried hard to avoid my whole life.

But they spilled out, anyway. I'd spent so much of my life being looked at but never really being seen or known. For a person with anxiety, losing control of myself and my emotions felt a lot like what I imagine it would feel like to be thrown into the deep end without knowing how to swim while everyone else at the party splashes around having fun. You are drowning and yet no one can tell.

Sometimes an undoing is the most important thing that happens to us as we remember who we are.

It was the beginning of a new baseball season, our second with the Boston Red Sox. Back at Massachusetts General Hospital, one of the best hospitals in the world, I parked my car in the garage and hoped to find some answers with a new fertility doctor. I took a picture of my parking spot so I could remember where I parked when I headed back to my car, which made me feel like a real adult who did wise things. Grief had matured me in an unwelcome but necessary way. Unlike the naive girl from two years earlier, who would have wandered around the parking garage lost, eventually needing to be rescued.

In some ways, I was comforted by the woman I was becoming; she was mature, wise, more aware, more empowered, and filled with the knowledge that life wasn't always simple as she once believed. My privileged life couldn't protect me from navigating a fertility journey, and it was shaking me awake. Eventually, I became more curious and less certain about life, God, and myself, and while it felt stressful and scary to no longer know what I believed, it also felt freeing.

I walked into the hospital all alone, which also felt like a big feat. Going places alone was something I struggled to do when my anxiety was at its peak. Living post-miscarriages brought on a new kind of anxiety, filled with fears that felt valid.

Would I ever become a mother?

Was something wrong with my health?

Do I have undiagnosed cancer?

I didn't have the energy to imagine horrific scenarios because I was living one. I walked to the elevator and headed to the third floor where I would meet Dr. Stephen to go over my latest test results. He was the best of the best. The top fertility specialist in the state.

As I sat in the waiting area, I thought, "Here I am, right where I never wanted to be but somehow deeply knew I would eventually land." Three miscarriages after finding out they don't do any follow up testing unless you've had three. Sometimes, I think our subconscious recognizes truth when we hear it, even if we aren't ready to fully accept it as truth.

I couldn't help but be slightly angry. Women's health is probably the least understood field in the medical industry, and it shows. I was starting to understand the deeply held patriarchal systems that uphold this country and the medical system. And yet, while I was thankful for all the interventions science offered, I couldn't help but wonder if I was just one big science experiment. After a year of being shuffled around from doctor to doctor and taking test after test, I could never understand why they never seemed to have any solid answers as to why I was miscarrying in the first place.

I had completed my last round of testing just a week before this meeting. I had a procedure to check on my fallopian tubes—to make sure they were open, so that I could hopefully avoid a future ectopic pregnancy. RR had done fertility testing too. He was thrilled to find out that his sperm count was *above average* for a twenty-seven-year-old male.

I sat down in Dr. Stephen's office in the beige color chair matching his beige-colored walls. Scanning the room, looking at the accolades, awards, and accreditations that had covered the walls. Dr. Stephen sat behind the desk, wearing his white lab coat with blue stitching of his name. The way he sat, he seemed to be welcoming me as a friend, but I was still on the edge of my chair with body language that screamed, "I do not want to be here."

"How about that game last night?" he started.

I smiled, half annoyed that he knew who my husband was and half relieved for the comment which lightened my anxiousness. I sat back in my chair and took my jacket off, realizing that I was going to be here a while.

"That was a good one, huh?" I remarked. I was an expert at making baseball small talk even though I hated it.

I had no clue what happened in the game last night. Not the score, who pitched, or who won. I had watched a thousand games before that one and could convince a grown man that I'd watched a game I hadn't; that's how familiar with the game I had become. But the deep dive into small talk sliced through my anxious armpit sweat like a sword.

"We can dial in Robbie on my office phone at any point you want him to be a part of this. We usually do these meetings in the patient rooms, but I thought we would be more comfortable here," he said.

One of the perks of being a baseball family was the special treatment. What I once felt guilty for having, in this moment felt almost deserved for having to do this alone.

"I will catch him up after the appointment."

RR would have been there, but I knew the drill for these kinds of appointments by now. You go over results that you only halfway understand that lead to more indefinite answers and follow up tests. I was hopeful for answers but knew I would rather share them with RR later when it was just him and I.

There is something unnerving about hearing about the status of your womb with a doctor and nurses surrounding you. My womb—a sacred space designed to carry life wasn't carrying life and became the topic of discussion with basic strangers, who were using language like *FSH levels are slightly decreased* to label and diagnose me. And nothing felt sacred about that.

I didn't want to be having this conversation with a doctor. I wanted to have a baby the old fashion way. Was that too much to ask?

"There is good news and bad news," he continued. "Let's start with the bad."

I held my breath, and made my lips disappear inside my mouth.

"Your labs all look normal and healthy! You do have a slightly decreased level in one of your egg counts in one ovary, but really that doesn't give me any concern for conception. Since you are young, we still have plenty of eggs to work with, but it is on the lower side for a woman your age. I like to see anywhere from twelve to sixteen follicles. You have eleven on one side and thirteen on the other."

This doesn't seem like such bad news, I thought. He paused, waiting for a response.

"Okay," I said, firmly nodding my head.

He continued, "Because we just do not know enough about the female reproductive system, we can't give you a conclusive answer as to why you have suffered in this way. We believe there may be genetic factors playing a role. After women have miscarried this many times, or they have been trying for over a year, or in your case both, we call that unexplained recurrent miscarriage and infertility."

I was annoyed that after a year of testing and meeting with some of the best fertility specialists in the nation, they could only give me a fancy way of saying, "We have no clue. You are a mystery."

So, you're telling me we have walked on the moon, we send people to space, and cars can supposedly drive themselves. But you can't tell me why I can't get pregnant and stay pregnant? Isn't a woman's pregnant body the single most important vessel in the continuation of humankind?

These thoughts ran through my head, but I didn't have the nerve to say it.

"You are a candidate for preimplantation genetic screening via in vitro fertilization, which leads me to my good news: IVF."

He went on to explain how many people he has helped become families and have children via IVF. I could tell Dr. Stephen had had this conversation with many women. He was proud of it. He got to provide the solution to people's heartache. I, however, was not expecting to hear that news.

I expected to get answers, but instead was diagnosed with a mystery. If the best fertility specialist in the country couldn't figure out why my womb was malfunctioning, what qualified him to know how IVF would even work for me in the first place?

Disappointed to say the least, I managed to get important words out. A question that had lingered in my mind for months.

"Can I ask you a question that has been weighing on me? Could this have anything to do with going to Africa during my first pregnancy?"

Dr Stephen clasped his hands and leaned forward, realizing that I was not so thrilled to hear what he considered good news.

"Did you get sick on your trip or get bitten by any mosquitoes?" he asked.

"No. I didn't. I drank clean bottled water. I didn't even brush my teeth with tap water. No sickness and no bites. I was vigilant." I said, feeling defeated from the memories of last year.

"You know, Brittany, my wife traveled to Africa when she was pregnant, and she was completely fine. Some doctors might suggest you not travel abroad while pregnant, but I have seen firsthand that traveling is not usually the reason for a miscarriage."

I believed him. His words were a gift to my heart. I needed to let myself off the hook even if only a tiny bit. My brain skipped back to IVF.

"Isn't there just a pill I can take?"

I just wanted to know why I was getting pregnant so easily, losing them, and then unable to get pregnant at all.

"Is something wrong with me? Can't you fix this with a pill? There has to be something easier than IVF?" I asked. Still hoping for some sort of quick and easy fix.

I knew dozens of women who had walked through IVF. Mostly other baseball wives who had walked the road of infertility before and shared their experiences with me. I held their hands as they wept, apologizing for their hormone-induced hysteria after a transfer didn't take. I had listened to the sounds of their cries when they received the same news I did. Enough women had opened up to me about the delicate process of IVF for me to know this was not a light decision.

"What are my other options?" I asked.

"Unfortunately, at this point, we don't have any other options. I am suggesting we do PGS, which is a genetic test to improve your chances of getting and staying pregnant," Dr Stephen said matter-of-factly.

"But we don't even know why I'm losing them. Couldn't I run the risk of going through all of this with IVF and lose them too?"

"Yes, that is a risk," he said, leaning back in his chair again.

"What are my chances of getting pregnant again with a healthy baby without IVF?" I asked, reaching for some semblance of hope.

"There is always a chance, but I believe this path will give you what you want the quickest and the safest way. Based on what I am looking at in your chart, your body just needs some help doing its job."

He said it in grace, but it stung like salt on a wound. *What my body was supposed to be doing, but couldn't.* I had already suspected my body was broken. And Dr. Stephen had just medically confirmed it.

Where is your good news? I kept wondering.

His energy shifted, almost like he wasn't used to getting the reaction I gave him. He was excited to present me with IVF as the solution. But I was just digesting that I was infertile and would never be able to have a baby the way I wanted to.

I looked up and asked, "Do you mind if I discuss this with my husband?"

Knowing I wouldn't be able to repeat all the things Doctor Stephen had just told me, we dialed him in. Robbie was at the field practicing before a game. He was in a different mindset. He was happy, chipper, removed from the situation. Robbie did what he always does—tried to find the bright side. He was hoping I would follow.

"Hey babe! How's the appointment going?" he asked, slightly out of breath.

Our energies didn't match.

"Hey. I am with Dr. Stephen going over some results that I want him to share with you."

"Okay! Are you okay?" he asked. I could tell he was worried, but still trying to sound positive.

"I'm fine." But I really wanted to break down.

I looked at Dr. Stephen and raised my eyebrows, letting him know to re-explain everything he had just shared with me. I'd already decided to be angry about this. Dr. Stephen explained everything to Robbie.

"Robbie, do you have any questions? Doctor says we can start IVF as early as next month when I start my period. All I have to do is come in on day one to three of my period and start birth control for two weeks. They already have your sperm, so we are good to go."

I hated every word coming out of my mouth. It was so robotic. Mechanical. Emotionless.

I went home and started researching holistic ways to heal your body of infertility, finding everything from losing weight, drinking herbal teas, to bigger deeper lifestyle changes like changing your drinking water, avoiding pharmaceuticals—specifically ones that have never been studied for the effects on pregnant women—eating organic and avoiding stress. It all seemed overwhelming and none of those things were going to help me get pregnant overnight or as fast as IVF might.

Avoid stress? How does one avoid stress if she can't just escape from life?

You never think it will happen to you, until it does. Infertility affects a growing number of women in the US, with an estimated 7.3 million women receiving fertility treatments.[3] By the time you read this, that number could be even higher. I had no idea it took so much effort to have a child. One out of four women will have a miscarriage in her lifetime, and yet, when it happened to me, I knew of no one.

For some women, all it takes is sex to have a baby. For others, it takes fertility medication. And for a handful of us, it requires a breathtaking miracle.

chapter nine
RUINED HOLY WATER

THE INFERTILITY DIAGNOSIS SHOOK ME to my core. I had come to terms with how I felt about IVF. We decided to move forward with it as soon as I felt peace about starting. But no matter how much I tried to force it, peace never came. Either I was traveling while I was supposed to go in to see Dr. Stephen, he was out of the office unexpectedly, or I got my period date messed up and couldn't get into the office. Though I couldn't explain it with words, my gut was whispering to wait.

As I waited to get my period each month, I started researching infertility and how the body gives us symptoms as a messenger to say, "Something is wrong!" I started to change my mind about something being wrong with me (shame) and started to believe nothing was wrong *with* me, but something was wrong. Infertility was a messenger: my body was trying to tell me something, and I was just starting to wake up to listen to it.

All these years, I struggled with headaches, poor digestion, heavy debilitating periods, and anxiety. I never realized that we aren't supposed to live in a state of constant chronic pain, numbing with over-the-counters and pharmaceuticals that are just band-aids for our symptoms.

And now infertility—the only thing that had the power to get my attention and wake me up. If we aren't investing in our health, we must be investing in our sickness. And my investments were revealing. But I lived, ate, drank, and consumed so similarly to everyone else around me. So I had no idea why it was only *my* body that seemed to be broken.

I am an Enneagram Four wing Five. The Enneagram is a system of personality typing that describes patterns in how people interpret the world and manage their emotions. Fours are individualistic. We live in our emotions, and when we feel secure and are healthy, we have a deep desire to be different than everyone else in the room. But the wing Five in me is the researcher. (Your wing is the number on either side of your main Enneagram type that is more dominant in your personality.) I use research to supersede my emotions when I can't see past them. My research opened the door of holistic health and the power of nature to help us heal our body. I went down plenty of rabbit holes about how essentially everything we consume in a standard American diet is poisoned with toxic chemicals, pesticides, heavy metals, and hormone disrupters.

Some of the research I found pointed to studies on long-term side effects of birth control. I had been on birth control for a decade from around the age of thirteen to twenty-three when I got off it because it was changing my personality. I originally went on birth control as a teenager because I had debilitating periods. I am talking staying at home for a few days a month in pain with bleeding that was so heavy I would pass out and get migraines, mood swings, and anxiety. Just to name a few. It feels crazy to even write those things out, knowing what I do now. Knowing it is possible to heal. Knowing how I determined all those things were "normal," and so did my doctor. But normal and common are not the same thing. And while those symptoms are definitely common, they are not normal.

Toward the end of a decade of being on birth control, I noticed that it altered my personality. I went from being a highly sensitive person to a numb, apathetic person. When I would accidentally forget to take the pill or skipped a day, I would have drastic mood swings. But I stayed on birth control because it helped my period cramps, cleared my acne, and my doctor told me to. (Insert the biggest eye roll you can imagine.)

After a decade of taking birth control, I stopped—it was too hard to fill the prescription while traveling so much—and waited to see if my horrible, no good, awful periods would come back. They did. My bad periods became horrific vengeful periods accompanied with anxiety and life altering migraines. I stayed off the medication because even when I was completely lost when it came to hormones and paid such little attention to my body, I knew it could not be ideal for the female body to be tricked into believing it's pregnant so it does not release an egg every single month for years on end. Altering the natural biological functioning of the female body, the female reproductive system, cannot be dismissed in the conversation about why so many women suffer with fertility issues.

In my gut I knew playing this decade-long trick on my body was a part of the reason my body said "no thank you" when it came time for me to actually carry a child inside my womb. I also did not set myself up for success by taking pharmaceutical drugs prescribed to me for traveling abroad (These have never been studied for use during pregnancy).

On top of it all, in middle school I fell into the same trap as many other girls and women, believing the less calories you consume, the healthier you are. The smaller your body, the happier you will be. If I could go back to my thirteen-year-old self, I would hug her and tell her to eat more than three grapes for lunch. I'd stop stepping on the scale every day and allowing it to determine my mood. I would tell my twenty-one-year-old self to stop taking birth control and get to the root cause for my periods being so bad in the first place. There's always a root cause.

But we can't go back in time. So, here we are. Deemed *Infertile*.

Birth Control was the first set of medications prescribed in the process of IVF. What a full circle moment in my journey of learning to trust myself again. With the unseen force that seemed to be stopping me from getting to my appointments, I think all along I could not shake the feeling that IVF just wasn't for me. At least, not yet. Not until I had more answers.

Naturopaths look at fertility as a sign of optimal female health. Let's not confuse that with the belief that having a baby defines your worth; instead, it's the idea that the female body was designed to get pregnant and birth babies if she chooses to do so. When that natural biological function is impaired, it is wise to start asking questions. Women are supposed to be able to get pregnant and sustain a pregnancy when we are fully nourished—not in a state of stress—and our hormones are functioning optimally.

I was back in India just a few months after my infertility diagnosis, and even though I was still reeling from Dr. Stephen's words and treatment plan, I couldn't help but feel Divine hope. I'd returned to the only place that felt like peace to me. Looking at the girls rescued by Nai Asha, I saw how powerful God was and the depths of despair and darkness that could be turned into stories of hope, survival, and resilience. Though our stories were vastly different, I couldn't help but think that if God could rescue Renu and the girls at our safe home, maybe God could rescue me too. That was the constant stream of thought running through my head. It was the dangerous hope that I held onto—dangerous because this kind of hope put everything on the line.

It was risky business to question everything I knew—or thought I knew—about God. After all, religion taught me that if I came to the wrong conclusion about God, my salvation was on the line. Yet I consistently saw the wonder and mystery of the Divine reflected in the work we did in India. God was active there, and I could access the Divine in a way that I couldn't seem to back home.

On this trip to India, I took another baseball wife, Ashley, and a friend, Courtney, who was leaving her role in the Peace Corps to sign on as Mission 108's director of operations. Her new position would free me up to focus on my health. But the truth was, I wasn't as concerned with my health as I was getting pregnant.

India was a welcome distraction from all the female fertility research I had been doing. Courtney jumped right into her role by flying from Ecuador to India to meet the staff and girls and see firsthand what Mission 108's work was.

Once we got to the safe home, I could breathe again. My body recognized this place as safe—just like the name says. But beyond that, there was no performing there. No one cared who I was married to or what I filled my Instagram squares with. The character I had created and the armor I wore back home and in my baseball life was non-existent and unnecessary.

Renu walked up to me the way a little sister would. For reasons only energy and the Holy Spirit can explain, I had become a safe place to her too. I wasn't in her daily life. We did not speak the same language. As far as I knew, she didn't know about the financial pledge that Mission 108 gave. It was her story of healing—despite death calling her name—that inspired me and made me better.

The first time I met her, she sat alone outside of the pack of other girls that formed their clicks. Even in the safe home, girls traveled together in packs. That wasn't just an American thing. But not Renu—she liked to be alone. Observe. Listen. She was wise beyond her years. Deep in thought almost always. We were similar in so many ways. Sisters in heart because we understood each other beyond language.

"Why do you people come here?" she asked. I knew what she meant. She meant, why would us Americans, who seemingly have everything, come to girls that society views a peasants. Trash, even. Untouchables, they were called.

Before coming to the safe home, she'd only known a village without clean, running water or air-conditioning. Her innate wisdom told her wealthy people don't usually waste their money or energy on the poor, let alone really see them, laugh together, or break bread.

"I don't know why others come, but I come to see you." I said.

She leaned her head on my shoulder, "But why?"

"Because I love you, Renu. I love you, and I want to see you. That's why."

"But why do you people come *here*? To see us?" She emphasized.

"I think there is an assumption that Americans have everything we need. And we do in some sense. We have so much more than we need. Our physical and financial needs are met. We have a lot of stuff. But we are missing *this*. What you and I have, doesn't exist much back at home. People in America have forgotten how to love. You remind me. We come here just to be with you all because you remind us of Jesus. You remind us what love is," I said.

Renu lifted her head off my shoulder and looked me in the eyes. She didn't say a word but smiled. I waited for something profound to come out of her mouth. But it didn't. That was all she needed from me. She picked up a stick from the ground and dragged it behind her as she walked away. I have no idea if she was still thinking about what I said or had moved on.

She is a child after all.

And I'd barely recognized her when I first saw her. Her cheeks were full, and she wore a constant ear to ear grin. Her hair was longer. Her limp was completely gone. She stood upright and was able to sit in a chair without pain. She was proud to practice English. The program was working. Love was doing its job.

* * *

I've talked a lot about yoga, and that's because it helped develop me as a woman, helped me learn how to be. I learned how to be connected to myself and sit with the questions I had about life:

Who am I?

What am I going to do with this pain?

Why does God allow horrible things to happen to His people, to children?

Instead of needing to find the answers right away, I was able to let the answers come to me, allowing God to reveal Himself to me instead of making God into what I wanted Him to be. Yoga taught me how to lead with curiosity instead of certainty and that small shift changed the way I live.

And Yoga Teacher Training taught me how to be a gospel witness. Evangelism taught me that there was always something to fix and perfect. But yoga taught me how to allow things to be what they are. Not try to fix them, perfect them, or be the savior.

In anti-trafficking work, there is almost an automatic, knee-jerk response to want to fix things. But there is no quick fix to trafficking and arguably, we will not see trafficking end in our lifetime.

Much of the work I do for trafficking survivors is at home and on a computer, networking and raising funds. My time in India was just about *being* with the girls—spending time with them, experiencing life with them. Being a witness to their lives. For the first time, I had to sit with the darkness in my own life and with the darkness of human trafficking.

The same day Renu asked why I was there, I planned to lead the girls in breathing exercises and yoga focused on releasing stored trauma in the body. In Yoga Teacher Training, there was such a strong emphasis on identity and purpose. We were forced to ask ourselves the hard question, "Who are you?" The girls had identities placed on them from the time they were trafficked. Slave. Unwanted. Servant. I felt there was no better way to speak into them and start with helping them understand their worth than by speaking life over their bodies as they did breathing exercises and released stored trauma.

Breathing exercises are beneficial for any type of trauma whether it be sexual abuse or any other kind of trauma (big or small) we face.

Believe it or not, the girls had never practiced yoga. Even though they lived in the birthplace of yoga, in many states and regions in India yoga is seen as a religious expression and isn't accessible to everyone. The irony of being an American teaching Indians yoga was not lost on me. I did my best to honor the practice and give credit where credit was due.

When I led the girls through the exercises, it was apparent to me how much trauma dissociates you from your body. I watched them, as I called out simple poses and saw them struggle to make the mind-body connection. At first, I thought it was the language barrier, but Vinita and my translator assured me it wasn't. Because of their trauma, they had dissociated from their bodies as a means of survival. Several of the girls had opened up to me that when they were abused or starved, they had to check out mentally and emotionally to get through the abuse.

The power our minds have over our body is wild. We can literally create an alternate universe when we need to in order to get through hard things. In some strange way, even though I would never understand even an ounce of their particular kind of trauma, I recognized that I too had learned to disassociate from my body in times of distress.

I told Vinita about my infertility diagnosis. She refused to accept it.

"You are going to become a mother. I know it. Infertility is not a title for you, from our God."

She would place her hands on my belly or my shoulders and say a blessing in Hindi. I believed her over anyone else even though the women in my life back home expressed a similar kind of hope. Her hope felt different.

Vinita's pastor also prayed for me and my womb. After I had seen my husband healed of his hernia, I knew miracles were possible.

Courtney, Ashley, and I pulled up at Pryanka's house where the pastor was scheduled to meet us. Pryanka is the first graduate of the safe home. She successfully took her parents (who trafficked her) to court and was one of the first victims in Northern India to win a case against her abusers.

Pryanka ran a beauty salon out of her home. When we walked in, she beamed with pride. She never thought she would live independently, let alone run a business. But this is what Nai Asha does. It gives new hope and new life to those who are rescued.

As she served us tea that she had prepared, the pastor walked through the doorway. The scent of chai tea—cinnamon and clove—filled the room. It had the perfect ratio of tea and buffalo milk. I can't tell you what it is about raw buffalo milk, but you have never had a creamier, more delicious cup of heaven until you have had buffalo milk in your tea or coffee.

As I sipped my tea, Vinita walked over with the pastor, explaining in Hindi the status of my womb. Pryanka took Courtney and Ashley on a tour of her home while I introduced myself to the pastor and thanked him for traveling to me.

Without hesitation, Pastor Daniel placed his hands on my forehead and started to pray aggressively in Hindi. He pressed my forehead with his hands to the point where I had to use my ab strength to keep my balance.

A smile came over my face, and I thought, *What have I gotten myself into?*

I kept my eyes closed and tried hard to hold back an uncomfortable giggle that desperately wanted to escape. Was I going to laugh out of discomfort or cry out of overwhelming emotion? Maybe both? I had no idea.

What the hell was happening to me? How far was I willing to go? I am going to freak out Courtney and Ashley, I thought.

The doubt and fear and embarrassment filled my mind.

I never felt more American in India than I did at that moment. If you're American, you already know this, but that is not a common practice back home in the evangelical non-denominational church. You might find that in the backwoods of Kentucky, in a traveling charismatic church, but this was not the norm for me.

After everything supernatural I had seen while traveling abroad—the miracle healings of my husband and Renu, the demonic oppression lifted off the girls in the safe home, and the medicine men doing witchcraft on children—nothing felt stranger than having a pastor that I did not know push on my forehead in the name of healing my womb.

I opened my eyes after a few minutes, and the prayer was over. I thanked Pastor Daniel and looked over at my friend Ashley, who had never been to church in her life, and Courtney to make sure they weren't too wide eyed or making an exit.

"Where is your water?" Pastor Daniel asked.

Confused, I confirmed with Vinita that he wanted my water, then I handed him my half-full water bottle, expecting he wanted a drink. But instead, he held it in both hands and said a prayer.

"Drink this. I blessed your water. It is holy water now." He handed it back to me with confidence this would work. He explained that many women in India come to him for healing and he has seen women who have waited up to fifteen years and then got pregnant and had babies. He smiled. I smiled. We both bowed with our hands pressed together in prayer position. He left the house, and I never saw him again.

No other instructions came with my holy water, so I went about the rest of my day like it was just another day, tucking my experience away to process later. India is full of life and adventure and experiences that take some time to process. I have often witnessed something in real time that I can't fully understand until I get back to my hotel room to journal or until I return home.

This was one of those things.

The next morning, without realizing it and still fighting the jetlag haze of the morning, I tossed my Starbucks Hibiscus flavor packets in my bottled holy water and chugged it down. It wasn't until I was on my way out of my hotel room that I remembered what I had done.

Did I just ruin my holy water with Starbucks Hibiscus green tea flavor?

Am I going insane?

Will it still work? I can't Google this crap.

Okay, Britt. Stop it. You cannot be so desperate to have a baby that you depend on holy water to heal you, and even if it does, the chemically processed instant flavor packets can't ruin it completely, can they?

Running late to meet the girls for breakfast, I rushed downstairs to have my morning cup of coffee with buffalo milk. I tried not to think about the fact that I might have ruined my shot at getting pregnant or that I might be losing my mind. I wanted to focus on my last day on the ground in India. After breakfast we went to the safe home to spend the morning with the girls and say our goodbyes. But before I could even leave the hotel, the only place I had WIFI, I got a call from RR.

chapter ten
FIVE-YEAR PLAN REVISITED

"I AM GOING TO HAVE surgery on my back the day after you get home," RR said. The time change from India to Boston, Mass was ten and a half hours. So, as he went to bed, I was starting a new day.

"They told me I would be begging for surgery when I knew I needed it, and today I was begging. I want to crawl out of my skin. I can't escape this pain."

I've felt like that before.

A few weeks before I left for my trip, RR noticed pain in his lower back. He had no significant injury except for dodging a line drive ball into the dugout where he landed on his tailbone. We assume now it was one of those injuries that happened over time, starting with the fall on his tailbone and then getting worse over the next couple of weeks of practicing, running, and pitching until he could barely walk. He herniated his L4 and L5 discs in his lower back and tried to do some non-invasive therapies to heal but ultimately needed and was begging for back surgery. Which is no small feat.

Surgery was not ideal at this point in his career. Surgery is never ideal, but RR was coming off of the best season of his career the year before, ending as the closer for the Boston Red Sox. This year was a building block for a long-term contract, which was the ultimate goal for any athlete.

He tried as hard as he could to avoid surgery, but a cocktail of narcotics weren't even touching his pain when I left for India. The fact that he called me to tell me a day before I was coming home let me know that this was only getting worse.

"I'm on so many narcotics to stop this pain and nothing is touching it," he explained. His Dad flew from Kentucky to Boston to be with him while I was out of town. He wasn't able to sleep through the night and could barely walk to the bathroom.

In the five days I was gone, things had gotten significantly worse. Crying over the phone, feeling guilty that I had left him in the first place, I just wanted to get home to my husband. I didn't even think about the ruined holy water until months later.

"I just want to be able to walk again," he said right before we hung up. I have never heard this man complain about anything. Most of my friends joke about their husbands' man colds and their not being able to handle a little sinus infection. Besides his hernia from years ago, I have never seen RR truly unwell or unable at any point in our marriage. Even when he got food poisoning from eating some sketchy gas station meat or a sinus infection, he'd power through like some sort of Viking. He'd tell me he was fine and smile even as he vomited up gas station hotdogs like an exorcism was being performed.

He is farm bred through and through. Farm people never get sick. And if they do, they, somehow, power through it. Growing up, little Robbie spent his days outside, hands in the dirt, climbing trees, creating a whole world for himself with his five other siblings on the back property of their farm.

When I got home, RR had the surgery on his back and went on, hopeful for a full recovery. We flew home to Kentucky before baseball season was over and watched the rest of the season from bed while he recovered.

* * *

A few months before the Holy water experience in India and the call about RR's back surgery we were standing in the kitchen of our rental home in Boston. We revisited the conversation of what our five-year plan was versus what was happening.

We always wanted to adopt. We imagined how we would walk through the adoption process and knew from the beginning, even when we were dating and dreaming up our lives, that adoption would be a part of our story. RR thought we would wait until after biological children or after we had a better idea of what his career would look like year to year. I wanted to start the adoption process once a healthy pregnancy came along, knowing how long adoptions can take and wanting our kids to be close in age.

When we were younger, getting to know each other like every new couple does, we went over every detail of how we wanted our life to look. He said things like play professional baseball, travel the world, and become a dad. I said things like travel, live in NYC, and become a mom. Over the years, we threw out random numbers of how many children we wanted before we knew what it meant to raise them. At one point, I wanted seven. At another point, I wanted ten. RR would amuse me and tell me we could however many I could handle.

We had a lot in common for what we wanted out of our lives. But the thing that stood out to me the most about him—and perhaps one of the reasons I fell in love—was his desire to adopt. We both wanted to adopt independent of the other's desire.

Adoption was always a part of our plan, but planning an adoption is sort of like planning out a baseball season. There are so many variables.

Eventually you learn to surrender trying to control what happens and trust that what is supposed to happen will.

When the healthy pregnancy never came, I started to wonder if I should continue to wait for a healthy pregnancy to start the adoption process. So, I asked my friends who had adopted what agency they worked with and to put me in touch with people and resources that would help me navigate the adoption process.

Something felt off about all the private adoption agencies I talked with. They were well oiled machines when it came to matching expectant birth moms to hopeful adoptive parents, and it almost felt like the tenderness of the nature of adoption was lost. Or at least, not what I had imagined. It lingered in the back of my mind, that some of these private adoption agencies felt more like legal human trafficking. If all bio mom needed was support, be it financial or emotional, then shouldn't we have agencies that only do that?

One night when RR was playing an away game, I opened my computer and logged into Facebook as I waited to see if he would get in the game. When I opened Facebook, I saw that I was tagged by two of my close baseball-wife friends, Jessica and Jenny, in a post about adoption: "Birth mom looking to place her baby with a black or mixed-race family at birth. Please contact the agency at the email below if you know anyone."

In the best of ways, I felt the little flutter of hope revisit me again. *Could this be my baby?* I reached out to the agency and expected to hear from them within the next few days. I had been emailing other agencies and found that they were pretty slow to respond to hopeful adoptive parents.

I heard back from the agency that night. Within one week we were (unofficially) matched with the expectant mother. A lot of agencies won't officially match adoptive parents with expectant moms until they are around twenty weeks pregnant. Jasmine was seventeen weeks along.

I booked a flight to Florida to meet her right around twenty weeks, when we would officially be matched as adoptive parents and expectant mother. I was there less than forty-eight hours to meet Jasmine in person to see if she wanted to choose us to adopt her baby.

And this was just one week before my second trip to India. We told no one. Not our family, not our closest friends. It was just between RR and me. A little (huge) secret to protect our own hearts and to protect our loved ones from more loss.

A woman from the adoption agency, Kristin, picked me up at my hotel, and we made the two-hour drive to meet Jasmine at a park with her two other children. I was anxious, wanting her to like me while also understanding this really wasn't about me at all.

Our small talk and conversation flowed effortlessly. I connected with her immediately. She asked me a list of questions about my family, how many children I wanted, how I would discipline, and how I would do the baby's hair—something that is sacred in the black community. Given that my hair is a mix between black and white, I knew why she was asking.

But it was her last question that made me anxious, and I remembered it the rest of her pregnancy.

"Can you place older children for adoption?" she asked. While Kristin, explained that yes, you can place older children for adoption, I looked over at her two kids playing in the dirt next to the picnic table where we were sitting.

Why is she placing her baby for adoption? I thought, but I knew it wasn't my place to ask. I wondered if she had support. Who was helping her raise her children? The biological father of her two older kids wasn't in the picture. The biological father of her baby in utero wasn't in the picture. And she had a strained relationship with her own parents.

Alternating between parts of my brain that were telling me two opposing things, I sat there and listened as she explained how overwhelmed she was. One part of me, the hopeful mother, longed to have a baby in my arms. But the other part of me, the part that was louder and stronger, thought about what would be different for her—emotionally, financially, physically—if she just had a little support. Would she be raising her baby if she had the resources she needed?

I hugged Jasmine as I left that day and wouldn't see her again until a few months later at an ultrasound appointment that RR and I got to join. That was when I looked into her eyes and saw an untold story. A story that I would never get to fully understand. Even though I wondered and deeply believed in Jasmine's ability to parent her children, I continued down the adoption path with her because I believed in her. I believed she would make the right choice for her—that wasn't a choice for me to make or try to influence. I also knew I was the best candidate to raise the baby if she chose adoption.

We left and I asked one million and one questions on the way back, making damn certain that this adoption was right for us and right for Jasmine. *Why is she placing for adoption?*

Does she have family support?

Do we know who the biological father is?

And so, I did the only thing I could do in this kind of situation: I prayed.

I prayed for Jasmine. For her baby. For RR's heart and my own. And I held two truths in the palms of my hands at once: I deeply wanted to be a mother, often it felt like at all costs, and I fiercely believe the best place for a child (with a few exceptions like neglect and/or abuse) is with their biological mother. And with more support from friends, family, and society women can mother their children best.

Adoption is not for everyone. It is for the called—the healed. The willing. The obedient. The open. Opening this door to adoption revealed in me that I am here to take the road less traveled. I wasn't certain where that road would lead. But I could clearly see that not many were willing to travel it.

Adoption is a beautiful and trauma filled story. For a birth mom, it is filled with loss and grief and ache. For adoptive parents, it is filled with joy and hope and trust and uncertainty and is one of the clearest pictures of the Divine I can fathom. The baby holds both tensions inside of her heart forever. At birth (or whenever separation from the biological mother occurs), a very specific trauma begins. A severing of *home.* The only home that baby has ever known was its mother. Regardless of whether that home was safe, the baby still recognized mom as safe. Babies are not meant to be separated from their biological mothers, where they're nursing, bonding, and being fed, loved, and comforted by the only person they've ever really known.

When that severing happens, a trauma occurs.

The goal is for adoption to fill a void where the baby was not receiving love, care, or nourishment. We as adoptive moms won't fill the void where the original trauma started, but that is not our job. We are not meant to replace anyone. In many cases, the void would've been there whether the adoptive mom stepped in or not. Our job is just to hold space for the void and love the children God gave us. But we cannot ignore the fact that a traumatic severing occurred.

I wrestled with this particular adoption story until the day the baby was born. With adoption, even if you are matched during pregnancy, the baby is referred to as the biological mother's baby until all papers are signed and the court/judge has approved adoptive parents as the legal guardians. This is wise for protecting the hearts involved, and, simply put: the baby does not belong to the adoptive parents until the law says so.

But that knowledge does not make the longing for your baby go away. If you're called to adopt, that longing likely won't be fulfilled until you're holding your baby. As a first-time adoptive parent, I didn't know what to expect or how I was supposed to feel. And mostly, I felt conflicted.

I want to be a mom.

Is this MY baby?

Lead with love.

But don't get too attached.

Yay! We are adopting.

Oh, but Jasmine could do this if she just had a little support.

We supported Jasmine during her pregnancy the way the agency instructed. We texted multiple times each week. I emotionally supported her the way I would a dear friend. There are strict rules in what you can and cannot do to support a biological mom during her pregnancy, especially financially speaking.

A few weeks after I got back from India, during the off season, RR and I flew to Florida for an ultrasound. Again, telling no one in our family what we were doing. We landed in Florida and drove to meet Jasmine.

I was familiar with the ultrasound room, but for the first time in a long time, I was a part of hearing the heartbeat of a baby that was healthy. No doctor would come in to deliver bad news. No ultrasound tech would get quiet as she saw measurements that indicated something was wrong.

This is how an ultrasound was supposed to be.

Except it also wasn't.

We saw a baby girl in Jasmine's womb moving around, sucking her thumb, and being the cute, sweet baby that she was. She was a big baby and Jasmine, RR, and I laughed about how cute chunky babies are. Jasmine said something about how she thought the baby would look like me and have my complexion. Which made me feel connected to her, like she chose me for that reason.

The tech printed pictures for everyone. RR and I took some, and so did Jasmine. It felt strange taking a picture of another woman's baby. But this was adoption.

On the car ride back to the airport, I decided to ask RR how he felt about it.

"Was that weird?" I asked.

"Yeah," he said and then paused. "But I guess that's just how it goes."

"The baby was so cute, even just looking at her on the ultrasound. I can't wait to see what she looks like." We drifted off into dreaming about becoming new parents and ignored the unspoken feeling that neither one of us were able to name.

I wasn't brave enough to say it out loud, but I couldn't help feeling disconnected. I felt that undeniable connection with Jasmine. But when I looked at the ultrasound screen and saw the baby Jasmine intended on placing in our arms, I felt little to nothing other than, "Aw, what a cute baby."

Something felt off. A connection with the baby was missing. But we thought maybe that was just the nature of adoption, so we wrote it off as nothing. And I shoved down my feelings because nothing about life seemed to be going the way it was supposed to be.

We walked through the rest of Jasmine's pregnancy with her texting and calling nearly every week. I was her support team. I encouraged her on days she felt like she couldn't be pregnant a second longer. I listened to her talk about her struggles and how hard it was raising two children alone.

Just a couple of weeks before her due date, she started to pull away. Deep down, I knew something was off, but I chugged along, waiting for her to go into labor so we could fly out and hopefully be there for the birth.

Then, a few days before the due date, Jasmine sent me a message that said, "I don't want Robbie in the delivery room with us."

My heart rate sped up. This was the first time I had felt the deep uncomfortable split between what the birth mom wanted and what I, the adoptive mom, wanted. I wanted him there in the room for the birth of our baby, but I had to respect her wishes. It made me sad to think that when we told our daughter about her birth and how happy we were to meet her that we would also tell her that her father wasn't there.

But the baby wasn't ours yet. This was Jasmine's birth experience, and I knew I had to respect her choices. And as a woman, I was really proud of her for standing up for what she wanted for her birth experience. So much had been taken away from her in the past. This was what she felt she wanted, and I respected that.

"Okay. I understand." I responded. "Hope you are feeling okay. I know the last couple of days/weeks can be really hard physically. You are strong."

I didn't hear back from her. And I had to tell Robbie. His reaction was almost numb. He wasn't thrilled, but he didn't seem sad.

What was he supposed to do? He sort of loses either way. If he was too sad, he would feel selfish. Of course he wouldn't be happy about this. So, he just sort of took the news the way he always does: in stride.

That evening after dinner, I went into my bedroom, closed the door, and cried out to God. I laid on my bed, staring up at the ceiling fan, feeling like God could not be more distant but talking to Him anyway.

"This is not my baby." I wasn't sure where the feeling came from. But somewhere deep down, I knew something was off. Being the emotional person that I am, I asked Robbie to join me in my meltdown. RR is always rational. He is not emotionally charged like I am. He assured me that everything was going to be okay. I was probably just having first-time mom jitters. He wasn't upset about not being in the room for the birth and even said, "This is going to be really special for you and Jasmine."

"Do you feel connected to this baby?" I asked RR.

"No, I don't, but I think that will come over time."

That night, I fell asleep with unsettled feelings in my heart. Part of me wanted to text Jasmine and say, "Jasmine, you can do this. You can parent your baby. If what you need is support, we will support you. But I know you can do this." Instead of sending the text, I fell asleep, hoping to have a clearer mind in the morning.

The next morning, I woke up thinking it was strange that I had not heard from Jasmine since her last text about not wanting RR in the delivery room. I logged onto Facebook and searched for Jasmine's name.

Her most recent post was a picture of a baby with a name, weight, and introduction to the world.

She'd had her baby the night before. She decided to parent her baby. Waves of conflicting emotions washed over me, and I tried not to attach any judgment. Something profound I learned to do in yoga was just allow my emotions to pass by like clouds. Because they will pass. And they did:

Shock.

Confusion, but a deep understanding that this was the right thing.

Pride.

Sadness.

But the judgment did come. Soon after the pride in Jasmine's decision washed away came the shame, grief, and sorrow for us. Yet again, I could not become a mother. How much time, energy, and money was I willing to throw away for nothing?

And I still had to tell RR.

Maybe I am just not meant to become a mother. God is so clearly shutting doors.

After the semi-shock settled, I walked into the bedroom where RR was still lying in bed and said quietly, "She posted a picture of her baby on Facebook with a name, weight, and birth announcement. I think she is going to parent."

He sat up quickly and opened his arms up to me. I crawled in bed and laid with him, just breathing.

"Are you serious?" he asked, knowing I would never joke about something like this.

I didn't say anything. I was uncertain how he would respond in this moment. Sad that I had led him down another path of hope, only to be let down? Angry that we spent a lot of money on adoption fees and a process we'd have to sort out later that day? Disappointed that God seemed to be letting us hurt so much?

But instead, he just had compassion for my broken heart.

The day flew by, and I spent hours on the phone with the adoption agency discussing next steps. I had not officially heard from Jasmine that she decided to parent, so we need to make sure that was her choice. Once the adoption agency got in touch with her, the plan was to make a new plan.

There were a handful of families the agency felt we could match with. We talked about fees and finances—all the things that make adoption feel so unnatural. I texted my therapist and asked her if I could have an "emergency session" that day. She quickly responded with a yes, and we got on zoom.

"Hi, Brittany. We have a lot to talk about today," Jeannie said.

Ready to spill out all that had happened, I dove right in.

"The adoption failed." I am using that term even though I don't believe adoptions fail, but I hope you know what I mean. I didn't wait for her to answer but kept going because I needed to get my pent-up feelings out.

"She posted it on Facebook and that is how I found out." I finished.

I looked at her hoping she would coddle me. She did, in a way, but she always asked the hard questions too.

"Brittany, that is a lot to take in and so hard to find out on Facebook." She paused. "What are you going to do if you don't become a mother?" Of course she spoke in her calm, therapist tone like she did not just say the one thing I had avoided asking myself.

"Well, I will be very angry at God," I said. I was honestly sort of annoyed that she would even go there.

"And then what will you do?" she asked.

"I will stay angry forever."

"Really? You think you have enough energy to stay angry forever?"

"I guess I wouldn't. But I would just bounce back and forth between mad and sad until I die."

As an Enneagram Four, when I am sad, *I am sad*. I can feel the depth of my emotions, pack up, and live in them until someone (me) is ready to dig me out of the dark hole I got absorbed into.

"Sad and angry forever, huh? Do you think there would be any room for joy in between the sadness and the anger?" she asked.

Ugh, I hate when she does this, I thought.

"Yeah, I am sure there would be. I remember thinking I would never be anything but sad again after my Gran died, and I do remember laughing for the first time."

"You have been in this pursuit of motherhood for a long time now. You have been trying with all your might. And I think it is time we ask the question: What are you going to do if you don't become a mother? Who are you besides someone who wants to be a mom?"

I hated her for asking it. I hated myself for not knowing the answer.

Who am I?

It was the same question I had been asked in Yoga Teacher Training years before and I still didn't know the answer.

"I am a soul just trying to figure out how to be human," I answered likely stealing that from something I found on Pinterest.

"I want you to take some time to figure out what that means. To figure out who you are and what you believe without spending all your time trying to become a mother. It will happen if it is going to happen. We need to focus on surrendering."

She made a fist with both of her hands and said, "You are walking around in life like this." She showed me her fists. "Let's try to just for a few moments a day walk around like this." She opened her palms.

She was right.

Whew. Sometimes we hear the truth before we are ready and want to reject it, but we can't.

I knew I would be more pleasant, and perhaps find joy, if I learned the art of surrender. It sounded good. That was the kind of woman I wanted to be. One who knew deep in her bones that life was happening for her not against her. One who carried herself with an understanding that living in alignment with your soul means surrendering what we think should happen to what does happen and having a deep trust in the Divine and yourself.

I just didn't know how. I wanted a recipe book. Steps to follow. Religion had offered me that once before, and I loved having that guide. But it wasn't working well for me anymore. *So now what?*

Once you lose your religion, a few things can happen. You either lose your way completely because the path without instructions is too much, too hard, too scary, or you find faith. You find a dangerous hope that only God can live up to. You find an unshakable trust in yourself and the Divine that becomes a dance. Only time would tell what path I'd take.

Drained from a day of phone calls with the adoption agency and a zoom therapy session, it was finally time to crawl in bed. It had been one of those days where you aren't quite sure how it happened. Like when you are driving home, arrive home, and wonder how many red lights you ran or how you even got there.

When I laid in bed that night, I felt an emptiness. Not a dark emptiness, but the kind that is ready to be filled up with something new. I was supposed to be a mother that day, and it didn't happen. My whole world was flipped upside down, and yet nobody knew except for RR, me, and a handful of people we named as references for the adoption agency. I knew going to sleep meant I would have to interact with my friends and family for the week and act like nothing big just happened. *More pretending.*

I grabbed my journal and sat with my thoughts. What came next had to be the Spirit of the Divine because it changed me forever.

Can you trust me in the darkness? I wrote.

I always wondered what people meant when they said they heard the voice of God. It was always something that separated me from the other Christians. I never felt like I could hear the voice of God. Or if I did, I couldn't distinguish his voice from my own voice.

If there was ever a time that I heard a voice that wasn't my own, it was then.

Can you trust me in the darkness?

The answer was clear: *No.* I didn't. I hadn't. But I wanted to.

I needed to be honest about that before I could make another choice. No, I had not trusted the Divine. I had used up all my own resources and depended only on myself.

I was out of options. I had tried every other way. I was drowning in the deep end of my life. Splashing, flailing, reaching, and swallowing water to try to save myself, denying I needed any help. But what I needed was to let the Lifeguard save me.

Okay, God. I will try to trust You. I can't make any promises. But I will try.

In the following days, I would hear that voice inside my soul again and again: *Trust me in the darkness.* And the next morning, I knew I was not capable of pretending anymore. I sent a text to my close friends and family that said, "Hi. Robbie and I were in process of adopting, and the woman we matched with had her baby yesterday. She decided to parent. We are heartbroken and devastated and wish not to talk about any of this until we are ready. Thank you for understanding."

After sending the text, I felt relief like I have never felt before. I was done pretending. I did not have one ounce of energy left to play the game of perfectionism—a game I was clearly not winning. I was able to let the people I loved, who loved me, see the real me for the first time in a long time.

RR sat with me on the couch and canceled his workouts for the day so that he could be with me.

"Britt," he said. "We need a break. You need a break. I need a break. I really don't want to talk about another baby unless by some miracle we can bring the baby home from the hospital *that* day."

I knew he was right. I was in full on "go" mode with the adoption agency trying to figure out the next steps when really what I needed was to fully grieve our losses.

Until that moment, I am not sure if I ever slowed down long enough to grieve at all. The losses rolled in so quickly and piled on so high that by the time I got back up, another one came.

I canceled my plans for the week and allowed myself to have simple daily routines that brought me joy, like drinking tea and cleaning my house. RR and I bought a hot tub, which became a place of healing for me. *Isn't it strange how bodies of water, even just a hot tub can create healing in our pain?* I submerged my body in the hot water in the middle of winter and looked up at the stars. The whole world is held together by a divine mystery. We think we know things about God, but we are really just guessing.

It wasn't the miracle of becoming a mother that I was after anymore even though I wanted that too. What I really wanted beyond it all was the miracle of knowing I am truly known, seen, loved, and cherished by the Divine. The miracle of being able to put my hope in the Divine and have Him show up in my honor and defense.

When RR said he didn't want to know about another baby unless we could pick the baby up that day, don't think I didn't consider doing that. My pursuit of motherhood had sucked nearly everyone who loved us into a pit of sadness with us. When we experienced a loss, they did too. That was the reason we hid the adoption process from everyone. I wanted to protect them from as much as I could. I wanted control.

As I started to grieve appropriately, I knew how impossible and inappropriate it would be to hide an adoption from RR until the day a birth mom went into labor, and we could just go to the hospital and pick her up. Things just don't work like that with adoption. It is a process. It takes time.

If God had not taken control of my heart, I might have tried.

But truthfully, there was something that wasn't settling well with me about the process of private adoptions. Especially with the way things went down with Jasmine. I was her support system. But why didn't the agency provide support any for her? Why wasn't there a better way to support expectant mothers? I knew my singular experience was skewing my perspective on all private adoptions, but I couldn't shake the feeling that a place that was intended to be good might actually be doing more harm than good.

I let it go and settled into my husband's arms to binge watch Netflix the night before my life would change forever.

The following day, I was driving downtown when my phone rang. It was the local adoption agent we worked with to do our home study, not the same agency we worked with in Florida where the birth mom decided to parent. I knew she had heard what happened and was calling to see how we were doing.

I sent the call to voicemail.

The voicemail banner popped up on my screen, so I listened to it before I headed inside to meet my family for the first time since I shared the news about our adoption.

"Hi, it's Leigh, from the adoption agency. I am calling to check on you all. I know these things can weigh heavy on hearts. I also have an interesting scenario I would like to share with you. A baby was born yesterday. I think she's a girl, but I'm not certain. I don't have many other details, but if we can get to court Monday, you could have a baby in three days. Call me back."

chapter eleven

HOLDING SPACE

THE CALL FROM LEIGH, our adoption home study consultant, threw everything into chaos. I was still reeling from my conversations with my therapist, where she asked if I could stay mad forever. I said I would be angry at first, but then I'd just be sad. And I was sad. I had shifted back and forth from sad to mad like a teeter-totter for over a year. Just acknowledging it out loud with her cleared space for me to invite in a new emotion that had previously been crowded out.

HOPE.

And the question I heard from the Divine about trusting Him in the darkness made me feel like light was beginning to glimmer. So, when I got the call from Leigh, even though I was weary and had every reason not to believe anything would come of it, I had hope. A different kind of hope that I know came from the Divine.

I am not talking about the kind of hope we see in movies, where regardless of the story line we know the ending. I used to cling to that kind of hope. Now I see it as an illusion of control, a drug. I would get a little hit of false hope to get me through to the next moment. But this new hope, this straight-from-the-Divine hope, is the kind found in the quiet moments when no one would blame us for giving up.

In my grieving, I befriended that false hope to get through each excruciating day. False hope had only been nothing more than a temporary distraction to shelve whatever feelings I was experiencing. Now, the hope I was feeling was reckless, holy, and came from somewhere deep within my soul.

All odds were stacked against me, truthfully. But this dangerous kind of hope kept me engaged; I wanted to wait and see how this all unfolded. From the time I got the call from Leigh, to my life today, that dangerous, reckless, holy hope that I held onto is still my favorite part of the story. It is the one thing that kept me alive. Present.

Holding onto hope makes for a fantastic story. But in the middle of a hope journey, you often question yourself and your sanity.

I waited for Leigh to call back with more details. I immediately thought of RR and how he told me not to tell him about another baby unless we could bring her home from the hospital that very day. That was his way of protecting himself from more heartache.

We could have a baby in a matter of days. This was close enough. I'd hoped.

I called him.

"Robbie. There is a baby in the hospital right now. We think she is a girl. We could bring her home on Monday if the court ruled in our favor." It was a Friday, and the baby had been born just the day before. Robbie was in disbelief. He half thought I was crazy, and half wanted to dive onto the crazy train with me.

"Britt, what are you talking about? What's going on?" I can practically hear him smiling as he talks.

I explained everything I knew, which was very little at that point, and we hung up, planning to meet at home later. That night, we got a message from Leigh asking if we can meet the baby's biological mom for breakfast in the morning. She saw pictures of us and wanted to meet us.

"Yes," I sent back immediately. "We will be there."

I went to bed that night with joy and angst and hope in my heart, like a child forcing herself to sleep on Christmas Eve but never getting into a full deep sleep. The next morning, I showered and brushed my teeth just like any other day.

Except today was different.

RR and I drove to the restaurant and met Leigh. We were excited but weary. So much was on the line. Mostly, our sanity and heartache. I was ready to jump back in my dark hole and stay there if this became another closed door.

As we sat down in the booth, I was gushing with emotion. My armpits were sweating, but I didn't care. It was the beginning of February. The skies were still gray in the morning and all throughout the day. But I had an inner sunshine.

At the restaurant, two hours passed, and the birth mom had not shown up yet.

"Do you think she is coming?" I asked sheepishly, feeling embarrassed as I realized how long we had been waiting. Leigh checked her phone. Her eyes got big as she realized it had been two hours since she last heard from Serenity.

"Let me call her," Leigh said, making me feel discouraged.

She stayed in the booth with us as she called, but after a few minutes, there was no answer. Leigh hung up the phone and sent her a text. I don't remember what she said, but I felt like I had dragged us into another hopeless pit of heartache. She wasn't going to show up.

We planned to leave, deciding that if she had not shown up by now, she wasn't going to. Leigh said that she would let us know if she heard anything and what the next steps would be.

I walked to the bathroom partially to regain my composure. I sat on the toilet feeling dead inside and feeling sorry that I did this to RR again.

When I walked out of the stall, I caught myself in the mirror. I placed my hands on both sides of the sink—a place I would usually avoid touching in a public bathroom.

Watching my chest rise and fall as I breathed in deeply, I noticed my eyes looked tired and had bags under them. I was bearing an untold story inside my soul. A story that at this point felt too riddled with heartache to be redeemed. A story that felt hopeless and embarrassing.

When I looked at myself in the mirror, though, I recognized someone.

Myself.

Somewhere beyond the bags and tired eyes and sadness, I saw a woman who was so filled with hope that she would stop at nothing to become a mother. Even if it meant I'd never become one. The thought of giving up on my child, a child I had never met, was more unbearable than the pain I felt.

How can this be?

The hole in my stomach seemed like an invitation to creep back into the dark mental headspace I had stayed in since my first miscarriage—really, since my Gran died.

You cannot pack up and live in this sadness any longer, BAR. (BAR, my initals, create the name I call myself when I need to be my own coach in life.)

Get it together.

The Enemy has no foothold over your life.

Darkness has no foothold over your life.

I repeated that mantra to myself as I walked out of the bathroom, toward the front door, trying not to break down when I looked in RR's eyes. But I didn't see him or Leigh. I guessed they went outside. I scanned the room as I walked to the front door, but stopped when I saw the two of them sitting back in the booth.

Maybe they had heard back from Serenity?

When I got closer to the booth, I saw Leigh and RR talking to a woman who was sitting with them. RR caught my eyes and waved me over with a big smile on his face.

I pretty much floated to the table.

"Brittany, this is Serenity," Leigh said.

I smiled and sat down in the booth, thinking one last time: *the Enemy has no foothold here.*

The next day was Sunday—supposedly a day of rest. But there was no rest happening in my house that day. We heard nothing from anyone all morning but were told we would get a call as soon as the court proceeding was over the next day. We were zero percent prepared for a baby. In the ten days after the first adoption failed, I had buried the idea of having a baby anytime soon. I had been hesitant to have any baby items in the first place, given the nature of adoption and our history with loss.

We had one package of diapers, a car seat, and a handful of baby onesies given to us by people who knew we were in the adoption process. There was no nursery, no crib, no formula—nothing. Turns out, babies don't need all that much.

Monday morning finally came, and our case was set to appear in front of the judge at 10:00 a.m. We were not allowed to be in the room, as it was only between the biological mom, her lawyer, the baby's lawyer, and the cabinet. In every adoption case, the baby is given a lawyer so that there is a fair court proceeding to determine the best place for the baby. The cabinet is a group of advisors that represents the government in a court proceeding. They are involved in adoption cases when a baby is going into foster care.

It seemed like a sure thing. *Why would anyone want to send a baby to foster care when that can be avoided?* But I wasn't naive anymore. I was jaded. I knew what could happen. Not a single thing is promised to us in this life.

I got a phone call around 1:00 p.m. from Leigh's cell phone. But when I answered, I heard Serenity's voice.

"Are you ready to pick up your daughter?" She asked me the single greatest question I had ever heard. In that very moment, I became a mother. Before I met my baby, I knew she was mine. Given to me by her birth mother to care for, love, raise, and live in awe of for the rest of my life.

In the biggest emotional release one single moment could possibly hold, I dropped to the ground in tears.

"Thank you. Thank you. Thank you," I repeated over and over until I could hear Serenity's tears too. We both wanted this for our daughter. We did not want her to go to foster care. We were a team of strangers, both advocating for our beloved baby— fighting for this new, little precious life.

"We will head straight to the hospital and meet you there." I hung up and called Robbie.

"Robbie, can you please come home?" I said in a somber voice not wanting to give anything away. He'd been thrilled when I told him about the potential for a baby just a few days prior. He said he had a feeling this was different.

I don't know how he knew but he did. He wasn't anxious. He wasn't freaking out. He was just calm. He knew from the moment we met Serenity that everything would work out.

I have always been intrigued by this kind of bizarre approach to life RR has. I have never once approached a life-changing scenario with ease. I always meet change with fear, panic, and nerves and think about the million ways it can go wrong. Maybe that's why we work so well together. He is the calm to my storm. The peace that keeps me grounded. He allows me to float ten feet above real life because he knows I will come back (and calm back) down in the end. And it is his belief in me that always brings me back to steady.

Because I was losing it. For the first time in years, it was a good losing it. Excited. Nervous. And praying that nothing out of left field would interrupt what was about to happen.

When we pulled up at the hospital, I felt like I was floating on a cloud. I saw Serenity from across the room and made a beeline to her. Time froze. Tears were streaming down my face, and my grandma's spirit filled the room.

I was holding onto my daughter in one hand and her birth mom in the other. I let go of Serenity as she fully placed our baby into my arms and gave me a nod that silently communicated a million different things.

I looked her in the eyes and made her a promise.

"I will raise our daughter the best way I know how. You've given me a gift. I will never take that for granted. She will always know who you are. I love you."

I handed her a gold bracelet made by my friend Cara and showed her the same one I was wearing. "Our baby has one too. When she is a little older, I will put it on her, and it will connect us forever," I whispered. No gift could ever express my love and gratitude for Serenity. I knew that and so did she.

RR and I named our daughter Gypsy Wade, after my grandma, Lucille Wade. When I look back at pictures from that day, my eyes sparkled differently. Maybe tears really are a baptism of the soul.

We surprised our families by showing up on their doorstep with our five-day old baby. First, we went to the farm to meet RR's parents. Then to my mom's, my aunt's, and later, we had all five of RR's siblings and many of our closest friends come to our house. We didn't tell them we had adopted a baby, but the look on their faces made it all worth it.

You can watch it all—the baby reveal and me telling Robbie our baby was ready for us—on YouTube. Bring tissues.

It was the happiest day of my life. The day I became a mother. But the reality was, we had to wait sixty days for the adoption to be finalized. My heart was already madly in love with my daughter while it was also breaking for her biological mom. If it was finalized, I would have the rest of my life to process the loss my daughter experienced on a subconscious level the day she was separated from her biological mother, a loss so deep I could never fully understand. I compartmentalized the brokenness of adoption and knew that I would revisit it another day. After all, I would have the rest of my life as a mother.

I will keep the details of my daughter's story private, as it is her story to tell. And while I know the best place for my daughter is with me, her mother, I was also sad and grieved for a woman whose life circumstances and choices led her to a place where she was unable to parent her child.

Adoption is both tragic and beautiful. One of the best things we can do to honor our children's adoption story is to hold space for the reality that on the best day of our lives as new adoptive moms, there is also deep loss for our child and their biological mother.

I will always honor my daughter and her birth mom by holding space for that brokenness and loss. That is what a mother does. She holds space for the broken parts while simultaneously creating a life of love, kindness, joy, and hope. Life and motherhood are both/and. We, as mothers, create space for both the brokenness and the joy. It is our duty and our honor.

Our daughter's adoption story will always begin with loss; the severing of a bond and connection between the first home my daughter ever knew; her biological mom. That will always break my heart.

But we also know brokenness is never the ending of a story covered in hope. Broken is not a title God gives us.

As you can imagine, it took days, weeks, and months to process all we went through. My journey to becoming a mother was a slow crawl on my hands and knees. I did not come out on the other side unscathed. Of course, now I can say it was all worth it—for her. That I'd climb any mountain to get to her.

But in a hope journey, when things feel hopeless and you don't know if you get what you are hoping for on the other side, it all feels too much to bear.

My body did not take nine months to prepare and shape me and yet somehow—between adjusting to sleepless nights and figuring out how to become a mother in such a different way than my girlfriends—it all happened so naturally.

I had a vision that put the past four years into perspective: I was standing at a glass wall, banging on it. On the other side of the glass wall was a man. He was standing at a table, with his back turned to me. I was trying to get his attention. He never turned around. I had been standing at that wall for many years.

I had tried everything. Yelling, screaming, crying, threatening, demanding, pleading—and nothing seemed to get the man's attention. He never stopped working at his table, never turned around, and I wasn't even sure if he could hear me.

Out of nowhere, I saw a woman appear behind the man and walk toward me. For the first time in years, I saw the man stop working at his table. The woman in the distance got his attention. I stopped banging on the glass wall to watch what was happening. As the woman walked closer to the man working at the table, I could make out who it was.

It was my grandma. She smiled at the man like they knew each other. I saw her nod her head in amazement over what the man was working on. I tried to get her attention and started banging on the wall again. But she couldn't see or hear me.

Suddenly, the man turned around and walked toward me. There was something in his hands, but I was still focused on my grandma. Oh, what I would give for just one more moment with her.

The sight of Gran got blurrier, and I longed for her to stroke my hair like she once did, to feel her skin, and to look into her eyes as she told me everything would be okay. The man was approaching me, stretching his arms out in my direction, holding what he had been working on.

It was a baby.

The man introduced himself to me as the Divine saying,

"She took time. Good things take time, my child. She is like an expensive bottle of wine; I couldn't rush the process. I don't waste an ounce of pain. I bottle it up and turn it into something beautiful. I was perfecting her. Here she is. She is yours. My darling Brittany, I have loved you so much. While you were tired, weary, disappointed, and angry, I was working on her. She is Mine, and I am entrusting her to you.

"My child, I have held you every moment you have ever felt alone. If you sit still, you'll remember and know. My heart broke when yours did. I have collected your tears and used them to baptize your daughter. She is anointed. Her life will move mountains, heal broken hearts, and give hope to the hopeless. The world will see her light and know that I am real and good and faithful. I worked on her day and night, just like I know you wanted. I orchestrated every second of every day that led us here. It was all on purpose. Her in your arms is a gift to my eyes. You will understand a fragment of the love I have for you when you look into her eyes and raise your baby girl. When it appears as if I have turned My back, remember this feeling and know I am making beautiful things out of the dust. This is what you've longed for. I am so delighted to deliver you the gift of motherhood. I have never and will never abandon you. She is Mine, and so are you. Now go and love your daughter."

chapter twelve

TIME TO HEAL

JULY 2018

I WOULD REMEMBER THIS DAY forever—the day we became a forever family. We were already forever in my heart. But we were scheduled to appear in front of a judge and make the adoption legal—our names on the birth certificate. No matter what, she was ours and we were hers. No more worrying, no more stressing, just love.

That morning, I woke Gypsy by singing *Good Morning Gypsy Wade* and opening the curtain to let the sunshine in. I picked out her outfit, a white romper with pink and green flowers and a maroon headband, knowing the pictures we took this day would be some of the most special pictures we ever had.

It was sunny and seventy-five degrees that Wednesday. On my way out the door, I thought about how my grandma used to post the weather to her Facebook page to inform her twenty-seven friends and family members around the country what the weather was like in Kentucky. At her funeral, I'd read the forecast at the end of my speech, the way she would have liked it. She sent the perfect weather to us for the perfect day.

If she had been here for this special day, I know she would have posted about it with pride.

The three of us—RR, Gypsy, and I—hopped in his truck to head downtown to the courthouse. And on July 11, 2018, we rolled Gypsy in her stroller into the courthouse— the same courthouse RR proposed in front of—to finalize our adoption. It was just as magical then as it was when he proposed to me.

Outside of the beautiful stone building is where I said yes to forever with the love of my life over a decade ago. Oh, how I had no idea what life would bring us. We parked the truck right out front and walked inside. We were greeted by our lawyers and about a dozen of our closest friends and family members. We made our way to the courtroom to wait for our turn. Family court isn't all sunshine and rainbows and that was very apparent when we got to the hallway waiting area outside of the courtroom.

The energy of the building was cold, stark, and dreary—unlike the beautiful sun that shone outside the window I kept gazing toward as I wondered what had brought these other people here. They were standing right next to me, and yet our circumstances seemed so different.

Were they behind on child support?

Were their rights to parent being terminated?

Were divorces being finalized for some?

Whatever it was, you could tell that they weren't as happy to be there as we were. But nothing could shake the joy we were exuding.

Josh, a family member who worked at the courthouse as a deputy, waved us in his direction, and he explained that the judge decided to hold the proceeding in the judge's chambers instead of the courthouse.

This invitation gave us a more intimate setting to become a forever family. Instead of being inside of a courtroom, where the energy was clearly less than thrilling, we got to go to a large private room and sit around a table.

Judge Mable greeted us as we walked into her chambers. It was like we knew each other. She hugged me tightly, and grabbed both of my shoulders. Then she said, "Congratulations, Mama!"

She looked at RR next. "How about those Sox last night?" she asked, laughing while she punched him in the arm.

I don't know why, but I imagined that this day was going to be tense. Like the judge was going to question me to make sure I was fit to be a mother, trying to find every reason I wasn't good enough for the job. Maybe there would be some surprise questioning or pop quiz that I might fail under pressure. I was so used to being blindsided by life. Still waiting for the other shoe to drop.

After all the adoption paperwork and inviting the state, adoption agents, and lawyers into our home, I felt like I was being monitored and had to be on my best behavior to be seen as "fit to parent."

Once Judge Mable set the mood of the room with her warm hug and baseball joke, my shoulders relaxed. There I was. Able to breathe again. The little anxiety I carried into the day melted away. I was back to being present in my body, and I had not even noticed that I'd escaped.

I looked into Gypsy's eyes, knowing this moment would stay with me forever. But my body buzzed with adrenaline. After we raised our right hands and swore an oath to our daughter, I wouldn't have to worry about a single thing. I would get to walk out of that courthouse with a load lifted off my shoulders.

We sat down around the long oval table with our extended family and friends quietly gathered around us as we presented our identification to the judge; affirmed our desire to parent Gypsy; swore an oath in front of our loved ones, lawyers, and Judge Mable; and signed the adoption decree.

We were legally a family. It was already official in our hearts. Our names appeared on our daughter's birth certificate. It was as official as official gets.

Thank you, Jesus.

We walked out of the courthouse as a family of three, and aside from having legal documents to prove we were a family, absolutely nothing had changed. I knew Gypsy was mine from the moment her birth mom called me and asked if I was ready to pick up my daughter. Not every adoptive mom gets the same kind of love and generosity from their child's birth mom. But I am so thankful for the question she asked that affirmed me as Gypsy's mother. It was never her responsibility to do that. And it is not lost on me what a generous gift that was.

Months passed, and I was still riding the wave of the magic of motherhood. Since I was a little girl, I knew I wanted to be a mom and that I wanted to adopt, and now I was living that out after a long and brutal yet beautiful crawl on my knees toward motherhood. It was upon me. I was in it.

How sweet it was.

January (and a new year) was approaching, which meant it was nearly time to go back to India. I had a trip planned before we knew we would be adopting, and I was responsible for leading a dozen Mission 108 donors to India on a cultural exchange trip.

In the past several months of parenting and loving Gypsy, RR had been home with G and I. After his back surgery, he did not get a call from the MLB to join a team like we expected. His not having a job was both disappointing and rewarding. We are very fortunate that he was able to be home with us full-time to be a dad and husband. After all, he had been working (more than) full-time since he graduated from high school.

The downside was that RR was experiencing his own identity crisis. In an odd way, it was comforting that we both got to discover who we were at the same time. We had each other to lean on while we were rediscovering life and what we believed. We both had to answer the question, "Who are we if he is not a baseball player, and I am not a baseball wife?"

Adjusting to a more normal lifestyle was easier on me than it was on him. Plus, I was fully absorbed in motherhood and starting to feel more settled in my sense of self. The luxuries of baseball are nice, but if you aren't ready for them, they can change you. And not always in a good way. The pressure had gotten to me in several ways. I'd lived as a baseball wife pretending to be the way I thought I was supposed to be instead of just being free. And being me.

But Robbie wasn't just losing luxuries. He was losing an identity. A calling. A career. A paycheck. Our livelihood.

His first love, baseball, had betrayed him in a way we did not see coming. When he got injured, he was coming off one of the best seasons of his career. We fully expected to be in baseball for another five years, hoping for a long-term contract in a city that we could make feel like home.

But that didn't happen. From the time he was a little boy, he'd poured every ounce of himself into the game of baseball. For the first time in his life, baseball was giving him nothing in return. I recognized he was going through an identity crisis because I had just walked through one myself. Remember my emotional struggle to answer the question, *"Who am I?"*

Who was RR if not a baseball player? Well, we were about to find out.

The upside of not playing baseball was that we got to establish the foundation of our family together. Honestly, there was nothing sweeter than that, and we both knew it.

Leaving Gypsy for the first time to go to India was not my ideal scenario. But I was thankful that RR was staying home with her. He usually traveled with me, but we both decided it was best for him to stay back this time.

Leaving Gypsy to go to India felt uncomfortable, awkward, and at times I felt intense guilt for leaving my baby without being able to explain to her that I would be back.

* * *

Ever since my Gran died, I randomly get these feelings that I call downloads. I am not sure if it is my grandma or the Holy Spirit sending me messages but regardless, I have learned to pay attention when they come. I feel His presence in nature and on my yoga mat. The Divine often reveals himself to me by using the number 108. It shows up when I need to pay attention or know I am on the right track. We named our non-profit Mission 108 for that very reason. There are 108 seams on a baseball. 108 is a holy number in India.

This particular download felt almost like nagging. There was no tone of voice attached to it. It was following me everywhere—both mentally and in the physical world. I was seeing it on everything. I thought about it constantly. And I could not shake off this download.

It's time to heal.

It's time to heal.

It's time to heal.

It was New Year's Eve, and as excited as I was to go to India in a few days, I wanted to talk to RR about our intentions for the year.

"What is your New Year's resolution?" I asked RR.

Neither of us had one. Resolutions always seemed to come from a place of unworthiness. And even when I did make them, I never made it past January. It always felt like resolutions insinuated there was this outside thing that we needed to fix or achieve to like or love ourselves. But it was a good way to start the conversation.

"I think I am getting some sort of mantra download. I keep hearing and seeing the word *heal*," I said.

"What do you think that means?" he asked.

"I don't really know. But I can tell it's something big. I think I need to heal my relationship with God. From there, all the other stuff will unfold, ya know?"

I had not thought about the infertility diagnosis in months. I had tucked it away and told myself I would focus on that later. I wanted to devote myself to my daughter. It was our time to bond and fall in love. When I got the download that it was time to heal, something deep within me knew it was about something so much bigger than healing from infertility.

We left the conversation somewhat open ended. I didn't have the words to explain what I was talking about. I knew the word *heal* was nagging at me. I knew I should pay attention. But I did not know why.

Days later, after New Year's Eve and that conversation, I left for India. On the flight over, I got violently ill. I am talking about the kind of illness that shut down my entire body. I slept for fourteen hours straight on the flight. I wrapped myself in a blanket burrito, closed my eyes, and was passed out before the flight even took off.

When we landed, I was covered in sweat, pale, swollen, dehydrated, and my stomach felt like it was in knots. I made it through customs in enough time to race to the bathroom to projectile vomit.

Something you should know about me: I will go to extreme lengths to not throw up.

I would rather staple my lips together than vomit, especially in a public place. But there I was in the airport bathroom in New Delhi, India, bowing to the porcelain god from God knows what virus I must have picked up on the way. Once, I vomited my guts out, I felt well enough to meet the team back at customs to help get them through easily and on to the hotel.

So much for healing, I thought as I loaded our crew into taxis and tried to keep my composure. But I was still shaky from throwing up and not eating for sixteen hours. Miraculously, as things often go in India, I somehow felt much better during the days we were on the ground there and spending time in the safe home. I spent five days in the safe home with the team, catching up with the girls, doing henna, and visiting the new transition home where some of the girls would live after the two-year safe home program.

On the second to last day of the trip, we took some of the recent graduates to a coffee shop called Sheroes that was completely staffed by acid attack victims. Acid attacks are exactly as it sounds—someone throws acid onto another person to hurt or kill them.

We sat in the outdoor seating area and pushed and joined the tables together to fit our large party. We brought the entire American team, the India staff, and four of the girls who were graduating from the two-year program and moving to the transition home at the end of the month.

Right by our table was a giant trampoline. Only in India. I know what you are thinking. There was a trampoline in a coffee shop? Yep. I have no answers except . . . only in India.

The Americans were eager to jump. It was the perfect opportunity to let loose and have some fun after some intense days in the safe home. One by one, each American piled on the trampoline, bouncing up and down like we did as children.

I looked over at Ruchi and Maya, two of the Indian girls who came with us. I met them during my first trip on their third day in the safe home. We were only used to seeing the girls inside the safe home. But since they had graduated from the program, it was a joy to get to experience life outside the safe home with them.

When I asked them if they wanted to jump, they shook their heads in fear but giggled at us silly Americans. I could tell they wanted to get on, so I hopped off and went to talk to them.

"Do you want to try?" I asked.

They continued to giggle, but didn't answer. Leaning in towards each other in embarrassment like girls often do.

"It looks like fun, doesn't it?" I nudged.

Maya, our oldest graduate, who was also pursuing her nursing degree, was the first to say yes.

"Have you ever been on a trampoline?" I asked her.

"No," she whispered, shaking her head.

I put my hand out and said, "Let's go!"

She followed me like she was scared her feet might touch hot lava. Tiptoeing onto the trampoline, she let out a squeal of excitement and fear. She couldn't believe herself. Her audacity. Her bravery.

"I've got you. I promise," I said.

She trusted me but not the trampoline. Over the next ten minutes, I stood back and watched Maya learn how to jump on a trampoline. What seemed like a simple childhood experience, was a profoundly emotional moment.

I hopped off the trampoline once she felt comfortable up there by herself. I turned to one of the Americans on the trip, Amber, and touched my shoulder to hers as we took in the moment. No one at our table could keep their eyes off Maya jumping on the trampoline. We knew we were witnessing something amazing.

With tears in her eyes and a smile on her face, Amber looked at me and said, "This is a part of her healing. She is learning how to trust her body again. What a gift we get to witness."

"It's like they were set free from the brothel two years ago but haven't felt free in their bodies ever since," I responded.

We both looked at each other and said at the same time, "I can relate to that." Not feeling free in our own bodies, that is.

There was a freedom about them that we all recognized when someone is doing something brave—craved even.

I looked back at Maya who was now jumping a foot in the air with uncontrollable laughter. In that moment, it seemed like time stood still. I felt like I was watching a slow-motion picture. Her with her hair flying above her head, arms flailing, an ear-to-ear grin with all teeth exposed, and joy exuding.

"Yes. This is healing," I said.

Amber and I smiled at each other and wiped our own tears. We felt so proud of Maya, the other girls, and ourselves.

What a gift to witness someone heal in real time. To see a moment in time where joy, laughter, and presence allows someone to transcend time and physically and emotionally heal. The girls in the safe home had learned how to escape their bodies as a survival mechanism. They mentally checked out of their bodies because they were raped by strangers over and over for years on end.

The body is incredibly intelligent and will always do what it needs to do to survive. And what an incredible survival mechanism to have—the ability to mentally escape a moment that painful. But the thing is, once you learn to escape like that because you have to, it becomes harder to stay present even when you are safe. To stay within yourself.

The more you escape from your body, the harder it is to come back. And since my first miscarriage, and before that if I was being honest with myself, I had been escaping too. Emotionally running away and never slowing down. And we cannot heal what we don't acknowledge. When we are not present in our mind, body, or soul, we aren't giving ourselves what we need to heal. Escaping had become so natural to me, I barely recognized when I did it anymore.

* * *

My yoga mat had become a place I learned how to reconnect with myself and the Divine. I'd learned more on my yoga mat about who God was than ever before. Religion wasn't the enemy, but I had grown past what the box of religion could offer me. I think about religion now as a box. It offers us such a beautiful starting point for a relationship with the Divine.

But eventually, if we are paying attention, we start asking questions that religion can't give us answers to.

The yoga mat helped me sit with the questions. Moving is the body's way of reconnecting.

A friend pointed out once that when Jesus healed people, He often addressed their physical suffering before He ever addressed their sin or spirituality. Perhaps, there is something powerful there. God knows when our physical needs are met, there is room for spiritual healing. Just as the girls in a safe home heal physically first and then feel safe enough to learn a skill or trade. We too must heal our bodies first; it is the gateway to being set free.

On my mat is where I began to heal. But it doesn't have to be there. It can be anywhere we feel most alive. Jumping on that trampoline allowed the girls to come back into their bodies. It allowed them to heal, experience joy, and be present. Perhaps the recipe for healing was getting back into my body instead of living so much of my life inside of my head. Movement is the medicine.

On the last day in India, I scheduled a cultural experience for the American team and Indian staff. We were going to visit one of the seven wonders of the world, the Taj Mahal. The night before the trip, after celebrating one of our team members' birthdays, I got violently ill again. I laid in my bed, shaking with illness. Pain had overcome every inch of my body. Courtney, the Mission 108 director, was asleep in the bed right next to mine. Poor Courtney. She did not sign up for that.

After hours of avoiding it, I barely made it to the toilet in enough time to let out the birthday cake and garlic Naan that I devoured the night before. It was the kind of sickness where things come out both ends, and you feel like your entire body has betrayed you. There is no semblance of humanity in your eyes—it's exorcism-type throwing up.

I laid on the shower floor, letting the water hit me in the back, and threw up for an hour. After the water ran cold, I found enough energy to crawl back to my bed completely naked. But I did not have enough energy to care about the scene that Courtney would wake up to—seeing my naked, wet body scaling the floor of our hotel room. I made it to my bed, and that's when it happened.

On top of the stomach upset, it felt like a head cold was setting in fast. I sneezed. And unfortunately for Courtney and myself, and for you dear reader (because I can't believe I am telling you this)—I sharted in the bed.

That was it for me. I was on the edge of death. *Nothing could save me*, I thought. This is how I would go. Either from a wild and rogue case of the sharts or from the embarrassment, this had to be the end for me. Bury me in satin.

I told Courtney to go on without me. I couldn't even control my bowels or stand up, let alone go on a four-hour bus ride to the Taj Mahal. Not with this level of body betrayal. She agreed to lead the team for me—and thank God for her.

How is this healing?

Off she went, and there I stayed. Between vomiting and feeling sicker than I had ever been, I wondered how I was going to make it back to the states on my flight later that night without sharting my pants again. Our scheduled departure was right after the team got back from the Taj at midnight. I had only hours to get my stomach under control. Or else.

The team got back from the Taj with stories and souvenirs, and ultimately, their whole lives changed from an extraordinary week in Northern India. Vinita brought me Ayurvedic medicine that stopped me from sharting again. A true miracle. I made it the entire flight home without pooping myself or throwing up. But still had so much to sort out about what it meant to heal.

And I was certain, based on my experience in India, that healing was not linear.

chapter thirteen

FULL MOONS AND HEART ATTACKS

HEALING HAD STARTED TO TAKE shape. Ease came. Less pretending, more surrender. Isn't it funny how learning the art of surrender changes things? I had tried to trick myself into surrendering many times before, but I always ended up back in the same place mentally. Not surrendered. And holding on for dear life.

But this time was different. I had let it go. People often say that adopting a baby leads to a pregnancy. I don't think that's true, though. At least, not true enough. And it's not fair to put that silent expectation on adopted children or families who adopt. Adoption is not a means to an end. But what is true is that God moves quickly when we surrender. When we stop white-knuckling the thing we want so badly, there is room for the thing we want to breathe.

I surrendered adoption, and Gypsy came to us ten days later.

I had surrendered pregnancy, refocusing my efforts on healing my body. Instead of trying so hard that my hair fell out, I just played with the idea of allowing ease. I'd given myself permission to let myself off the hook for a bit, admitting that I'd been through enough emotional exhaustion to last a lifetime. My mornings were filled with drinking tea, playing with Gypsy, organizing our house, and allowing whatever came to come.

On an average sunny day in May, right after Gypsy's first birthday, I woke up feeling off. A feeling I had felt before. My stomach was bloated. My boobs hurt. I was ravenously hungry. Irritable beyond belief. And one thing was missing.

My period.

The morning went by. We spent time with family celebrating my niece and nephew's birthday. But on the way home from the party, I couldn't keep it inside a second longer and I blurted it out to Robbie.

"I think I need a pregnancy test," I said, allowing those words to settle.

"What?" Robbie asked.

"I need a pregnancy test," I repeated. "I don't feel right. I have felt this before."

"No, Britt. Your period is a few days away," he said confidently. He always knew when my period was coming better than I did.

"I know. But I am telling you I just need one."

"Okay. I'll go get one after I drop you and Gyps off at home," he said, half indulging me and half trying to gauge how serious I was. I was infertile after all.

"I am only that ravenously hungry when I am pregnant," I said.

We pulled up at the house, and I took Gypsy inside and laid her down for a nap. By the time I was done laying her down, RR was back with the tests and had laid them on the kitchen counter. I didn't see Robbie, so I grabbed the box and went to the guest bathroom where he wouldn't find me.

I peed on the stick and within seconds saw two pink lines.

Shock, joy, and disbelief washed over my body. I floated into the master bathroom where Robbie was and without planning anything sweet or cute,

I shoved the positive test into his hands while he was sitting on the toilet.

I grabbed my phone and caught his reaction.

"No way! No way! Are you kidding me? Is this for real?"

I was crying with my hand over my mouth, still in total shock.

"Why would you tell me this while I am on the toilet?" he asked jokingly. If you know us or follow me on Instagram, you know that Robbie spends most of his free time sitting on the toilet, so it likely comes as no surprise to you how I chose to tell him I was pregnant for the fourth time.

For three days, I allowed myself to be happy. Overjoyed. And then the anxiety set in. Anxiety that I could not shake no matter what I did. No matter how hard I tried, I was in it. Fear had me in its grip. I was right back where I was in the beginning. Scared to the point of no return. It wouldn't be long until I escaped my body again.

What am I going to do if this baby doesn't make it?

I went to my first appointment with a broken spirit and heavy heart, worried about my baby and myself.

I had just crawled out of a dark place, and felt like I was on the path to healing, now I was certain this pregnancy would end and set me back. I wanted to be excited about being pregnant again, for the fourth time. But I couldn't find an ounce of hope inside of me to believe this baby was going to be okay. That's the thing about hope. Once we feel like giving up, we are often faced with opportunities not to. That is what makes having hope so dangerous. It holds all the potential to let us down.

Trying to avoid devastation, I prepared myself for the worst. After all, the worst had already happened to me before. We had not been doing anything to prevent pregnancy because I believed the doctors when they told me I wouldn't be able to carry a child to term. Years had passed since my last pregnancy, so I just believed I couldn't and wouldn't get pregnant. I was not tracking ovulation or paying attention to my fertile windows, but we weren't trying to prevent a pregnancy.

"If this baby doesn't have a heartbeat, I am refusing to leave the office until they give me a D&C," I told RR on our way to our first appointment.

He agreed by shaking his head and reaching for my hand as he drove us to my appointment.

A D&C (dilation and curettage) is the dilation of the cervix and surgical removal of part of the lining of the uterus and/or contents of the uterus by scraping and scooping. It is the same procedure as an abortion except one baby has a heartbeat and the other doesn't. I had never opted to have a D&C after my miscarriages because it has the possibility of hindering your ability to carry successful pregnancies in the future.

But this time was different. I was done and not willing to carry around death inside my womb a second longer than I had to.

"I want my tubes tied if this doesn't work out. I can't go back into the dark hole I was in before." Barely allowing him to get a word in edgewise, I asked, "How did we even get pregnant?" My emotions were starting to get the best of me.

"I know, babe. I understand." he said back.

He didn't crack the joke I thought he would. RR is usually the hopeful, positive one. This time around, he wasn't hopeful. He was scared. He didn't admit it, but I could tell. And that made me even more worried. Previously, he was my optimism. I was the realist. I borrowed his optimism when I needed it most. But we learned very quickly in our marriage that optimism is often rooted in fantasies; it was hope that we needed and couldn't seem to find.

We know how this ends.

Just a few days after the positive pregnancy test, I got my naturopathic test results back that my progesterone levels were dangerously low. Too low for a woman that isn't pregnant. And I was probably six weeks pregnant if we did the math right. Meaning without my progesterone levels rising as they should in early pregnancy, I could start bleeding any moment and lose the baby.

Six weeks pregnant without the adequate amount of progesterone will terminate a pregnancy without a doubt. Low progesterone is one of the leading causes of miscarriages.

I knew I was in trouble. And so was my baby.

I was already devastated, and I hadn't even confirmed the miscarriage yet.

At the appointment, I settled my legs up on the table, lying on my back, and rolled my leggings down and waited for the cold gel like I had before. By this time, it was routine. I knew the drill.

I was at a new midwifery clinic in my hometown—one that all my girlfriends with babies suggested. It was a positive change after seeing OBs for most of my pregnancies. It was warm, family centered, and welcoming. I wasn't treated as a number or even a patient. I was treated like a mom who was scared to lose her pregnancy. Scared to lose her baby. I was treated like family.

The ultrasound sound tech put the scanner on my belly and started taking measurements. Within seconds I saw it. The baby. Right there on the screen.

MY BABY.

The tech hadn't paused long enough or turned on the sound yet, so I couldn't tell if there was a heartbeat. But I could hear mine. I turned to RR and reached for his hand. We squeezed each other's hands, and I felt the cold sweat of anxiety roll down my sides.

The ultrasound tech calmly entered measurements that I didn't understand. I wasn't used to this kind of causal energy at ultrasound appointments. Her face didn't look like anything was wrong. Usually, the ultrasound techs don't hide their shift in energy well when they scan a uterus that is supposed to have a baby with a beating heart inside.

There is an emptiness inside a womb with a dead baby. And this wasn't that. I could feel it. There was life inside of me.

She turned on the doppler. I closed my eyes as tears ran down my face and listened to the sound of heaven: my baby's heartbeat.

Lying on the table with the crinkly paper under me, I closed my eyes and took in the sound of a strong, healthy heartbeat. This is a magical moment for a mother.

RR and I let go of each other's hands, and I covered my mouth with my hands and opened my eyes.

"The baby's alive," I whispered to the tech, myself, and RR.

"Yep! And you are eight weeks, not six," she said confidently.

"What? No way!"

"Two weeks more pregnant than I thought!" Somehow, that gave me more peace. I was closer to the second trimester, which gave me some hope.

The tech gave me a cloth to clean my belly. I rolled up my pants and waited for the midwife, Dee, to come in. When she walked in and sat down, she introduced herself and smiled, bypassing my hand and reaching for a hug. She had tan skin, dark hair, and an energy that communicated she loved what she was doing—working with birthing women. I loved her already. She must have read my chart because, unlike the OB's I had seen in the past, she looked at me in my eyes when she spoke and cared that I was scared.

"We are going to take this pregnancy one day at a time. The truth of today is your baby is doing good. Okay?" she said reassuringly.

I nodded, and wiped a tear from the corner of my eye.

She built an instant trust with me within the first conversation. I trusted her with my pregnancy—and more so with my heart.

We left the midwife clinic that day with a dangerous kind of hope in our hearts that maybe, just maybe, this would be the one that stuck. It felt dangerous because that is what real hope is, isn't it? It is dangerous to have hope in something we want but know is not certain. There are no promises in hope. We do not get to know the ending until we arrive. We risk our hearts breaking, disappointment, and potentially being faced with what to do with our current belief system if our hope falls through.

The next morning, I woke up with a pain in my chest and I couldn't breathe. I gasped for air but couldn't get any into my lungs. My hands were weak like I couldn't make fists. My heart raced, beating so loud I could hear it.

When I started to get out of bed, I noticed I had blurred vision and tingling in my hands and feet. I walked to the bathroom, touching my hand to the side of the bed to guide me and for stability. Struggling for breaths, I bent over and went into the fetal position on my bathroom floor. I'd been here in this position on the bathroom floor with every single miscarriage. The bathroom floor. My darkest hours. I struggled to breathe for what felt like an hour, but time told me it had only been minutes.

The episode passed just as quickly as it came.

That week, every morning around the same time, the feeling would return like gusts of wind taking me over with no control. I'd place my hand over my heart, bend over in pain, and struggle to breathe.

Am I having a heart attack?

"It feels like the most violent adrenaline rush you've ever had," I told RR after an episode that week.

"Something is not right."

I had an appointment with the midwives the following week, so I waited it out to see what they thought and hoped the feeling would go away.

Before my next appointment, with the midwives, I had a therapy appointment.

"Chemical panic attacks," my therapist, Jeannie, said over a zoom call.

"So, I am not having a heart attack every day at the same time?" I was relieved, but still worried.

A chemical panic attack is when "the hormone adrenaline floods into your bloodstream, putting your body on high alert. Your heartbeat quickens, which sends more blood to your muscles. Your breathing becomes fast and shallow, so you can take in more oxygen. Your blood sugar spikes."[4]

The best way to describe it is to imagine the feeling you get when you're driving and slam on the brakes to avoid getting into a wreck but don't hit the car in front of you. Right after that, all your adrenaline rushes through your body and you can barely see, breathe, or function. Your heart is racing. You barely feel like you can move or grip the wheel.

That was exactly what was happening to me. It wasn't a heart attack, but it felt like what I imagine one would feel like. Every day for the remainder of my pregnancy, I had a chemical panic attack. And they got longer and less predictable, making every day of being pregnant a horrible one.

I'd always imagined that if I experienced a miracle and somehow got pregnant again, I'd be running through fields of wildflowers singing the praises of the Divine for healing me. And as much as I wanted that to be the case, it wasn't.

Chemical panic attacks were different than my usual anxiety. Pre-pregnancy anxiety was purely mental. I was able to work through that anxiety by using tools that got me out of my head and into my body. I could use logic to reason with my anxiety.

Chemical panic attacks felt more of a physical manifestation of anxiety in my body. They weren't anxiety in my head or emotions. They were felt and experienced in my body in a way that was crippling.

Jeannie suggested that, instead of running away from my anxiety and panic attacks, I sit with them. Trying not to avoid them but allow them to pass through me. Welcome them. In one of our sessions, Jeannie said, "And when they are over simply ask, "What are you here to teach me?"

I had always looked at anxiety as something that needed to be fixed. I had run from anxiety throughout my entire life. I'd been taught to medicate, fix it, avoid it at all costs. Anxiety takes a different shape when we allow it to be our guide. Just as infertility is a symptom signaling to us that something is not right, perhaps anxiety has a purpose too. We aren't meant to live with dis-ease in the body. But I was starting to see that the way to "fix" it wasn't necessarily always the way I'd been taught.

I knew I couldn't escape this feeling as much as I wanted to and as hard as I tried. The more I tried to avoid these panic attacks, they worse they got.

Yoga taught me how to breathe and move through moments of distress. But I couldn't practice yoga at all. I didn't know it yet, but I had severe anemia. Which made simple things like walking to the bathroom feel like I was dying.

In hindsight, not being able to practice yoga left me with only a few options. My breath and prayer. When nearly all my regular healing practices like yoga, the sauna, and long walks were taken away, I was forced to reconnect with the Divine and depend solely on grace.

Breathwork didn't make the episodes go away. To be honest, I am not sure if it really helped the episodes get any better. All I knew was that if I didn't close my eyes and breathe through them, allowing them to stay as long as they needed, they got far worse.

I searched for peace in my body during my first trimester, but all I could find was presence. Accepting that, for reasons I might never understand, I was going to have daily chemical panic attacks for the foreseeable future.

Because I was walking a healing journey and felt like I had taken so many steps forward—and was experiencing the miracle of pregnancy after loss—I felt ashamed and angry that my first trimester was so hard. And with the lingering feeling that I could lose the baby every day, I wished that things were different.

I arranged my days around the episodes in fear of being alone with Gypsy while I was having one and not being able to care for her, as she was only one. I avoided driving in the mornings because that is when they mostly happened. Sugary foods like honey and fruit seemed to be a trigger. And drinking one hundred ounces—not an exaggeration—of water before 10 a.m. helped keep them somewhat manageable.

My first trimester was crippled with fear and panic attacks, and Darkness did everything in his power to lay claim on my life. The story in my head became what felt like a reality. And I was convinced through dreams and visions that I was going to die during this pregnancy.

* * *

At my next appointment, I saw a new midwife. She was an older woman with gray hair and wisdom that came with attending many births.

"How are you doing and feeling? Let's talk about your mental health," she said confidently.

"I am just scared every day the baby is gone. That the heart isn't beating." She had the wisdom of a grandmother but not the empathy.

"Oh, you are twelve weeks pregnant. You are in the safe zone."

I paused. "Well, the thing about fear is it doesn't care about safe zones. And it certainly doesn't play by the rules," I retorted.

Her eyebrows raised with a little bit of shock. I stayed quiet, wanting her to realize I wasn't looking for shallow well wishes. I was in the trenches.

That's the truth. For someone who is walking through a hard season, the last thing we need is for our pain to be minimized. We know things work out the way they are supposed to. We know relaxing and having hope and believing for the best is so important. We know having anxiety and fear doesn't change the outcome. But sometimes, what we need in order to heal is to just feel the fear we have instead of dismissing it, shoving it down, or minimizing it.

Thirteen weeks rolled around. I had never been pregnant longer than this. Emotionally speaking, this was a big week for me. The panic attacks persisted. But by now, they'd become a regular part of my day, something I expected.

A full moon was approaching. My girlfriend, Amber, was holding a full moon circle at her house. I had never put any weight into the meaning of a full moon, but I had heard that women are their most fertile on a full moon and that was precisely when I'd conceived this baby.

A full moon circle is, "a sacred gathering of women, who usually come together to [honor] and celebrate the new and full moon. In ancient communities, this circle was used to call in the divine feminine, and as a way of grounding, centering, and receiving higher wisdom."5

Christians can get touchy about things like this, but the way I see it, I am not referring to the moon as my God. I am just confident that God put wisdom, beauty, and sacredness in the sun, the moon, the stars, and all of nature. And I think it is incredibly beautiful to connect back to God's creation.

I didn't have the wherewithal to wear pants or be out of my own home late at night, so I held a ceremony for myself in my bed instead of going to Amber's house.

I wrote down my intentions for the pregnancy, lit a candle, and prayed for a healthy and safe pregnancy. There was nothing woo-woo or witchy about it. It was simple. Beautiful. Intentional.

The thought, "A healthy and safe pregnancy with this baby" reverberated through my soul as I remembered what I had written on my vision board at the beginning of the year before I was even pregnant. I was entering the second trimester of pregnancy. New territory. New hope.

After I wrote out my intentions and was drifting off to sleep, I heard the still small voice that I understood to be the Divine, connecting me to my baby for the first time. I felt strongly that this pregnancy held the power to heal generations of women in my family. Generations of abuse, neglect, abandonment, fear, anxiety, and depression.

When I look back in my family lineage of women, there are generations of mothers unhealed of their wounds from these cycles. It was as if my ancestors' despair lived in the cells of my body, and I could feel it all boiling to the top as I carried this pregnancy.

If I gave birth to this baby, would it unlock a power inside of me that would allow the generations after me to be set free? Healed? Wild and free? It was that night with the full moon that I understood what it meant to heal and why I was on this journey.

All along, I had thought healing meant getting pregnant or fixing my anxiety. But in that moment, when the Divine connected me to my baby for the first time, I knew healing was so much more than anything external. I believed for a moment that this pregnancy held the power to release me from the entanglement of fear that had griped my life, so that I could live wild and free.

Healing my womb was a part of the journey, but so was healing my heart. My mind. My ancestors. My trust. My nervous system. My relationship with others, myself, and with God.

I did not need to just heal my womb. I needed to heal everything, so that I could be free again. I just had to get through the next two trimesters and see this whole pregnancy through. I needed my baby's heart to keep beating.

And the very next day, I felt my baby move inside my womb for the first time.

chapter fourteen
GOODBYE RENU

"RENU IS DECEASED. She unexpectedly passed away during a visit with her family due to neglect and possibly abuse. We are heartbroken. Please keep us in your prayers."

I received the email from Ashish, the director of operations at Nai Asha. Sitting in my living room, my body melted from the couch onto the floor, and my tears immediately began to hit the rug beneath me. I cupped my face with my hands, feeling a panic attack coming, but soon sorrow took over. I wept in a way that I had not wept since my Grandma died.

None of the girls in our safe home had ever passed away. We didn't just call Nai Asha a safe home because the girls were protected from trafficking, we called it that because they were safe with us. In our care, with Vinita, Ashish, the staff, and the security. How was it possible that we created a sacred home filled with nourishment, love, joy, and restoration for these girls to have a second chance at life, and then life was taken away from one of them? Renu, my warrior.

We created safety for them in a world that was too dark and too broken to care for them. And one of them, my precious Renu, was no longer safe.

She was gone. I had created a false narrative that God had rescued all of them for a purpose, and He did, but the illusion that nothing else could happen to them was gone.

Feeling my belly tighten, I instinctively reached down with one hand to hold my belly. My baby. The maternal instinct to protect my womb in the presence of danger, fear, cruelty—even if that danger wasn't directly affecting me or my baby—kicked in.

There was something unexplainable about the connection between Renu and me. Imagining the pain, neglect, and abandonment she must have experienced felt too difficult to bear. Knowing her death was a direct reflection of neglect from her family, but more so neglect from a society that outcasts and abandons the poor, made me sick. There was something about Renu's death that made me think of my own daughter. How we can be victims of our circumstances and wondering, once again, how God could allow this to happen.

I was worried for my baby but stuck in the pain of my heartache.

Gasping for breaths as the panic attack settled in, I didn't even have the wherewithal to comfort RR, who was sitting next to me watching this unfold. *How many times will he have to watch me break?* I wondered.

He looked down at me with concern but was sort of used to this scene. Although it looked the same as my usual panic attack, it felt much worse. Deeper. Harder to control. This one hit me like a wrecking ball. I felt almost lifeless.

"Are you okay?" he gently asked me.

"She's gone, Robbie. She's gone." I wailed.

"Who's gone? Who?" he asked in a more panicked tone.

I flashed back to the moment I told him that my grandma was gone and remembered how devastating it was. *Another loss. Why?*

"Renu died in her parents' care. She was home with them. This is my fault. I should have done more. I should have done more to protect her," I said.

My heartbeat calmed as RR helped me back up on the couch. I'm not sure how long he held me, as I caught my breath and wiped my tears.

Renu's case was complex because she wasn't staying in the safe home for a traditional human trafficking case. She was there on grounds of neglect and abuse which made her more vulnerable for being trafficked. So, the Indian government would not permit her to stay at Nai Asha longer than her two-year program without an attempt at reintegrating with her biological family or her living on her own and working—even though we knew neither of those options were best for her.

The staff and I were in the middle of month-long conversations about what was best for Renu, how to abide by the law but still support Renu and give her the life she deserved. The truth was she wasn't ready for either. There was a financial struggle in getting Renu's business started in a sustainable way, and we were hoping for funds to come through. Even still, she wasn't physically ready to live on her own. On top of that, she did not want to leave Nai Asha. The girls were her sisters. Vinita was like her mom. Ashish was like an older brother. Nai Asha was her home—the first home she ever had where she was safe and loved.

We knew placing her back at home with her family was not the safest place for her, but our hands were tied because of the law. The hope was that a short visit at home would give us time to set her up for success. But time was not on our side.

Renu became sick when she was back home and had similar symptoms as when she did when Vinita found her in the hospital. Renu's family lived in a rural village without access to healthcare, transportation, clean water, or adequate food. Whether her family intentionally neglected her or whether the neglect was a reflection of living in extreme poverty, we don't know. And likely never will. But what we do know is that extreme poverty often keeps people physically and mentally sick.

I only have pieces of information from the day Renu passed away from Renu's family that were translated to me through Vinita and Ashish. I know she fell ill. I know she was throwing up blood the day before she died—the same thing that happened to her in the hospital when she was given weeks or days to live. I have pieces of the story, but nothing about her death will ever make sense. I am not sure what about death ever does.

But the same could be said about her life, too. Her life was a miracle. She was left for dead and supposed to die. Vinita nurtured her back to health. Nothing about that makes sense.

What I can tell you is that a parent should never be in a situation where they do not have adequate access to care for their child. Even though I intellectually understand the complexities of poverty that leads to neglect, my heart can never understand. And what a privilege that is.

It goes without saying that Renu's family lived in extreme poverty both physically and financially. But it is the mindset of spiritual poverty that takes over and can affect any one of us.

I have cried out to God asking why Renu died the way she did. I have blamed myself. Her family. The government. But the blame never replaces her, and I have had to wrestle with that. You know we often say that someone who dies young is gone too early. It feels comforting in some ways to believe that, but I am not sure it is the full picture.

Can we really lose people too early?

Too early for my liking, yes. For my comfort, of course. We have such little control over our lives and what happens between our first breath and last, but I am even more convinced that birth and death are mysteriously out of our control.

Renu's life started and ended in trauma, neglect, and abuse. Much of her story is plagued with a darkness that doesn't seem fair. Not all stories have happy endings. Some only have happy middles. Renu had a happy middle. I am sure of that.

After the initial heartache of losing Renu, my body stored the loss and used it as fuel for more fear to carry throughout the days of my pregnancy. The story I was telling myself was that everything goes wrong. As much as I wanted to enjoy it, I couldn't find my way. I didn't want it to be that way, but it was. I wondered what would happen to the baby with my growing stress. Stress isn't good for mom and baby, but I couldn't escape it.

In therapy, I discovered that I was entangled with fear. If it wasn't obvious enough, I realized that God does not intend for us to live with a spirit of fear. I did not just have a few fears. I had accepted and aligned myself with a spirit of fear and taken it on as who I was.

Fear of dying during labor.

Fear of losing my baby.

Fear of being seen as less than perfect.

Fear of not being enough.

Fear of abandonment.

Fear of failure.

Fear of success.

Fear of losing my religion.

Fear of LIVING.

Fear of losing myself.

Perhaps what I have been trying to heal all along is the relationship I have with myself and the Divine. Trying to wrestle with the question, "What do we do with all this god-forsaken pain?" I've lived with so much fear since I was a little girl, and it all came crashing down in this pregnancy. It forced me to take things one day at a time, to stay in the present moment dealing with my fears and living on nothing but a prayer. The things I had been running from were the very things I needed to heal.

What does it mean to lose yourself? I am not sure if we really can lose ourselves. We are right there all along, aren't we? But we can forget. We can forget who we are, and we can struggle to remember.

I didn't know it yet—but this was my remembering. My re-membering. When we remember, we dig into our past; we make ourselves aware of something or someone we've known or experienced as a part of our story. And that was the problem, the root of all my fears: I had lost awareness of who I was, and I was struggling to get her back.

To re-member.

Weeks later, Vinita flew into Kentucky to be with us for a fundraiser held for Mission 108. It felt nearly impossible to host a fancy gala while pregnant and having just lost Renu with no real goodbye. But I was happy to have Vinita by my side.

Vinita had not been to the states in years. Many of our donors hadn't met or spent time with her. After losing Renu, we felt this trip would be the perfect thing for both of us.

Vinita sat across from me at my dinner table and that familiar feeling of peace that I couldn't find anywhere else welcomed me like a hug from above. She wore American clothes instead of her Sari. Her long brown hair was in a braid and red lipstick stained her lips. It was nice to see her on my territory for the first time, but Vinita carried the feeling of home with her wherever she went. She brought bags of tea, spices for chicken tikka, jade bangles, prayer shawls, and jewelry for all her American friends and family.

One night, Vinita cooked an Indian dinner for Courtney, Amber, and me at my house. Vinita's garlic Naan alone is a slice of heaven. She sat at my dinner table after having hand-made the most decadent Indian meal and held Gypsy in her arms, stroking Gypsy's forehead as she fell asleep. Gypsy had never fallen asleep on anyone but me.

I want what Vinita has, I thought.

I watched Vinita, studying how she existed. The way she served, loved, moved, breathed, talked, and engaged others. I supposed I embodied those things too. But the thing she had that I didn't was that she didn't allow fear to be the boss of her.

One time when Shabnam from the safe home ran away, Vinita rescued Shabnam directly from a pimps home by knocking on the pimps door and demanding for Shab to be released. Shabnam was one of our sweetest girls—naive and just wanting to be loved. When she ran away, the staff heard that she had been re-trafficked by her pimp. When I was told about what happened, I sadly believed Shabnam was gone forever.

But not Vinita.

Vinita walked miles to the pimp's house and demanded that Shabnam be released. Was Vinita scared? Probably. But she carries Light within her, and she knows the Light always wins. Somehow, no matter how much darkness Vinita encountered, she still believes in the Light. And that belief allows her to let Light guide her instead of fear.

Vinita brought henna with her from India. She opened the package and offered to henna my pregnant belly. Henna is traditional Indian body art often used for decorating the body in big celebrations like weddings, pregnancy, or just because you feel like it. Life is meant to be celebrated.

As she hennaed my belly, I saw a new tattoo she had that wasn't there last time I saw her. Tattooed in red ink on her hand was the word, "REJECTED." It was made to look like someone had stamped it on her.

"What is that? Is it new?" I asked.

"Oh yes. I am rejected where I am. You know . . . because of the work I do. Because of God. Because I believe in the Light. I tattooed it on my body. Just to simply say, yes, I am rejected. I am proud of that," she said.

I sat there and thought about what it meant to embrace rejection for a moment before responding. Vinita was right. She was rejected. By society. By her friends. By her family. Even by her own culture.

In this world, not of it.

Working with women who have been trafficked in India is like working with women wearing the scarlet letter. She is looked down upon, an outcast. Growing up, she was rejected by her family for having darker skin than the rest of her family members. Now, she is a woman who fights for women's rights and works with those society calls the least.

Of course, she wants to be rejected by society. Society has lost its way. When a society or system is built upon hate, discrimination, and marginalizing people, I, too, would want to be rejected by it—wanting nothing to do with the way that system functions. Perhaps all of my dis-ease and fear came from trying to belong in a world I do not belong to. The discomfort I feel in the world is not because something is wrong with me. It is because something is wrong with the world.

Later, I looked up the definition of what it meant to be rejected. One meaning is "to refuse to agree to." Vinita refuses to agree to the ways of the world. She walks in alignment with the Holy Spirit and with her own soul. Of course, she is full of freedom and not fear.

It made me think about all the labels I had been given and even given myself. What stories I had been telling myself based on those labels.

Broken.

Afraid.

Alone.

Unable.

Hopeless.

Fearful.

There is a sacred divide in life where you only know the version of yourself that you've created. You meet the you that the world reflects back to you. Somewhere along the way, I had come into agreement with lies about myself.

Remembering back, I saw my divide happened in middle school when an older student stood before our lunch table with a chocolate teddy graham in one hand and a vanilla teddy graham in the other and proceeded to smash the chocolate one.

"This is what I'm going to do to the two Niggers in this school," he said for the entire lunch table to hear.

How does an innocent little girl react when she meets a cruel, cruel world? Often, she shrinks. She disappears. She runs. And escapes. And before long, she loses all her hope.

I wasn't free in my mind, body, or my soul. What needed to heal in my life became clear to me. I didn't just need to heal from infertility; I needed to heal from the lies I believed about myself too.

That's freedom. That is healing. To reject what society offers us and to have hope in something bigger than ourselves.

Until the pregnancy was over, I would battle these fears. The only way to the other side of fear is through it. I could not outrun the fear of losing my baby or myself.

Would I lose myself in loss again? Or did this pregnancy hold the keys to unlocking my freedom? Freedom from fear. Freedom from anxiety. Freedom from pressure to be perfect. Freedom from religion. Freedom from the chains I put on myself. So that I could finally be the wife, mom, and woman I wanted to be. So that I could be wild and free.

chapter fifteen

BIRTH, RE-BIRTH, AND RE-MEMBERING

JANUARY 2020

I STOOD IN GYPSY'S BEDROOM, rocking her to sleep as tears ran down my cheeks and hit my sweet girl's forehead. Tears are holy. I remembered my vision of Gypsy's anointing by the Divine and couldn't believe I was here. A mother.

"Are you ready to have a sister?" I asked my almost two-year-old daughter.

Everything was about to change. No matter what happened in my labor and delivery, soon things would be different. I kissed Gypsy goodnight and left the room wondering if these contractions would be the ones that ushered in my labor.

The contractions started earlier that evening as we walked around Target. I bought a pair of pink baby shorts and diapers. It was the first thing I had allowed myself to buy for the baby. Nearly the entire forty-two weeks, I believed on a deep level that one or both of us was not making it out of this alive. I bought them with the depressing thought that if something happened to the baby, then at least I would have one thing to remember her by.

It didn't help that when I shared with RR the dark thoughts of death and dying that I was having, he had been having them too. The Enemy had done everything possible to rob us of the joy of the miracle of this pregnancy. No one could fathom the daily internal turmoil I experienced—constant thoughts of dying during labor, losing the baby, or both.

"We want to induce you right at forty-two weeks," the midwives told me at my forty-one-week appointment. I was torn between my fear of stillbirth and the logic that babies don't come on their due dates, they come when they are supposed to.

I was at forty-one weeks and three days, trying to avoid the mounting pressure put on me to get this baby out. It felt odd to me to try so hard to keep her in for almost ten months and now I had to do everything to get her out within a few days. Pretending like I had control over any of it, I did all the natural crunchy things to encourage labor: Essential oils, evening primrose, walking, pumping, tea.

The baby was happy where she was and there were no signs of labor until that night. So, I dropped into my breath and practiced the techniques I learned for when labor started. Like you already know, I use research to ground myself when my emotions get the best of me. I had done an insane amount of labor research to prepare myself for this moment.

Surges of power ran through my body just like I expected. They would come just as quickly as they went—just like the miscarriages.

I remembered the women in my family as I pulled out my phone to time contractions. My mom spent twenty-four unmedicated hours in labor with me. Doctors didn't believe her when she went to the hospital and said she was ready to have me. They sent her home, and she almost had me on the hospital floor. My grandma, whose births I knew very little about. My daughter's birth mom, who chose life and adoption and me. I thought about my mother-in-law, who birthed seven babies and only had six earthside, as one wasn't born alive. I thought about my own three babies that never made it into my arms. I wondered how much my own birth would play a role in my birth experience.

Each breath and each contraction brought my baby closer, and despite all of the fear, I was doing my best to stay in my power. There was no turning away from the moment I was in. I was in labor.

Leading up to my birthing time, the past four years became clearer and clearer. I was on a journey. The journey was my slow crawl into motherhood, but bigger than that, this was the journey of rediscovering myself, my soul, the Divine. Each time a woman becomes a mother, I think she is also given the opportunity to heal a part of herself and become freer.

To heal is to pursue thriving at a physical, mental, emotional, and spiritual level. To heal is to live in alignment with your soul. One of the most healing times of a woman's life is when she transforms from woman to mother. I got to do that once through adoption, and I was about to do it again through giving birth.

Who was I about to become?

When a woman gives birth, she not only honors the woman she was, but she also finds within herself a new woman. A mother. A warrior.

Each time a woman gives birth to someone or something new—an idea, a dream, a baby—we heal the divine feminine power inside of us that the world, society, and even we have tried to take away, diminish, or corrupt.

In her book, *When the Drummers Were Women*, Layne Redmond says, "All the eggs a woman will ever carry, form inside of her while she is a four month old fetus in the womb of her mother. This means our cellular life as an egg begins in the womb of our Grandmother. Each of us spent five months in our grandmother's womb and she in turn formed within the womb of her grandmother. We vibrate to the rhythm of our mother's blood before she herself is born."[6]

My pursuit of healing was not just to heal myself. It was to set the generations after me free from the bondage that my ancestors endured. I was not only healing myself, but I would also be healing the generations after me, and possibly the generations before me.

When I look back at my generational line, I see women who fought hard so that I could have the life I do. It is not lost on me that the only reason I have the space to create healing for myself is because of the sacrifice they made. My pursuit of healing was for the women in my family line who were abandoned, neglected, abused, and especially those whose names I will never know who lived as slaves.

* * *

Surges of power ran through my body as I continued to time contractions.

RR fell asleep early that night, unlike his usual midnight bedtime. I supposed subconsciously he was preparing for birth too. I was thankful to be left alone to be with myself as I paid attention to every detail of my body and the early stages of labor.

I was quiet, focusing on every little detail that my body was feeling.

"Wake me up if you need me, okay?" Robbie said, as we laid in bed that night, knowing our lives were about to change.

"I will, babe. I love you," I said.

There was an unspoken fear in the bedroom. Neither of us had the courage to say aloud how terrified and overjoyed we were to be reaching the end.

RR drifted off to sleep as I sat up, trying to get to sleep, trying to breathe through a tightening feeling in my belly and avoid the horrendous heartburn that had snuck back in during my third trimester.

RR and I had never loved each other like this before. This was the definition of in sickness and in health. I wasn't sick in the traditional sense. But pregnancy had taken every ounce of energy I had. RR was picking up all the slack. Cooking all the meals, managing most of the day-to-day needs, and giving Gypsy the extra attention that I felt guilty not being able to give her.

In my second trimester, I was diagnosed with severe anemia. Trips to the bathroom felt like I had just run a marathon. When I stood up or walked too long (even just around my own house), I had to sit and take breaks because I would black out. On top of the daily panic attacks, I was not well. As much as I hated to admit it, afraid of sounding ungrateful, pregnancy didn't turn out to feel as amazing as I anticipated.

I thought without a doubt that if I was granted the miracle of pregnancy, especially after all that I had been through, I would embody that of a goddess. Unfortunately, I felt and looked like a tired orangutan stuck behind the glass at the zoo. You see this wasn't just my pregnancy. This was my community's pregnancy—and everyone was watching me navigate this miracle. I had shared my entire fertility journey on Instagram. People were praying for me. For this. And when I shared the news of being pregnant with my friends, family, and online community, it felt like their miracle too.

Chemical panic attacks and anemia, combined with the guilt of not loving pregnancy like I thought I would, did not add up to goddess status. But I was proud of myself for simply surviving. Sometimes we don't get what we want, but we always get what we need.

Laying down in bed made my cramps turn to stronger, more powerful surges that ran throughout my body. Those powerful surges led me to my bathtub to submerge in warm water. So, I filled the tub with warm water and essential oils. Once a surge would come, I stopped, closed my eyes, and went into another state of consciousness, breathing with intention. I put on my meditation tracks and filled my mind and heart with positive birth affirmations. I would give anything to live those early moments of labor over again. It's the beginning of transitioning, uninterrupted, beautiful, sacred.

The time had come.

I filled and refilled the bath with hot water to keep my body relaxed. The water didn't slow the contractions down at all. If anything, they intensified. I texted my doula at 2 a.m. while RR was still fast asleep.

"My contractions are three minutes apart, but I want to make it to 5 a.m. before you come," I texted her.

"I can be there in an hour. Whenever you are ready for me," she replied.

Bless my sweet little heart. I remember thinking that maybe I would have a baby by morning. I moved from the tub to the bedroom when I could no longer time my own contractions and felt like I needed more support from RR. I opened the door to the bedroom and heard RR still snoring.

A tiny inkling of doubt almost stopped me from waking him. I wasn't even sure what I needed from him. I just knew I needed a witness. One of the greatest expressions of love we can give someone we love is to simply bear witness to their pain, their discomfort, their transitioning. Change is vulnerable. Hard. Scary at times. Especially for those of us who love control.

Waking RR up felt brave to me. I was asking for the support I knew I needed even though there was nothing tangible he could do for me. I kept the lights dim but tapped him on the shoulder.

"Hey, I think it is happening. I have been in the bath for a couple of hours," I whispered.

He bounced out of bed like he thought he had missed it.

"Are you okay? How long have I been asleep?" He asked loudly.

I was still able to giggle at him, which gave me the clue that my labor was progressing, but I was not close to birth.

"The contractions are getting stronger and stronger," I told him.

"Okay. I'm here. I'm here for whatever you need," he said, trying to wake up from a dead sleep.

His presence was comforting. He brought me water and my yoga ball to bounce on. He squeezed my hips and rubbed my feet.

In the bedroom, I bounced on my yoga ball and felt the surges of power running through my body with smaller breaks in between. These contractions were working to bring my baby earthside with every passing birthing wave. I had to remind myself of that truth as each one felt harder to get through. One minute suddenly started feeling like ten. RR took over handling every detail of my needs, as I was no longer able to talk through contractions.

My doula, Hope, arrived then. RR must have called or texted her at some point close to morning. For me, time stood still. I had no idea I'd been contracting throughout the entire night or what time it even was.

I didn't see my doula's face until a few hours after she arrived, when the sun came up. The bedroom was dark and peaceful, and I wanted to give birth right in my bed but fear of something going wrong would ultimately transfer me to the hospital.

I was feeling a drastic change in the stage of my labor, but I couldn't identify what that meant. *Is it almost time to start pushing? How many centimeters am I?*

All the labor questions swirled around in my head, but I had no answers and no time to think as contractions felt seconds apart with no break in between.

"Are you feeling pushy? Like you want to bear down?" Hope asked.

"I think so, but I don't know," I responded.

I felt a lot of pressure, like the baby's head was pushing on my pelvis, but I had never experienced any of this before, so nothing felt certain. The pain of miscarrying felt similar to the sensation of contractions in a physical way, but the emotional experience was much different. There was a hope behind every contraction and knowing that each one brought me closer to my baby. The hopelessness of a miscarriage is just that—hopeless and empty. You subject yourself to pain and misery only to walk away without a baby in your arms.

After just a few intense contractions, I quickly said, "I want to go to the hospital." But even then, there was a still quiet voice inside of my head saying, "You can do this at home."

On the way to the hospital, the contractions nearly went away. I kept my sleep mask on, trying to create as peaceful of an environment for myself as possible. My birth training taught me that labor can stall in any transition where the body senses fear. It is a freaking amazing thing that God gave birthing women.

If I was giving birth 200 years ago, the way my ancestors did, I would likely be at home. I imagine I'd be in a village with other women who had given birth—they would be my midwives. If out of nowhere a lion entered the village and I needed to flee for safety, my labor would stop. Adrenaline would kick in and my body would naturally produce a hormone called cortisol that would literally stop my labor from progressing. The body is incredibly intelligent. If only we never lost our ability to trust ourselves.

The problem was that I wasn't being chased by a lion. I was just going to the hospital to have my baby. But the body recognizes an adrenaline rush in the hospital experience: getting in a car, bright artificial lighting, dozens of people poking, prodding, and asking you questions, signing paperwork, and so much more.

After a couple of hours of wishing for my contractions to come back, there they were again as strong as ever. I labored for over twenty-four hours in the hospital as my uterus contracted, and I danced my baby down and out. My body was doing exactly what it was created to do.

There was a moment when I stood in the shower in my hospital room—letting the water hit my back, hoping I was transitioning from 8 or 9 centimeters to meeting my baby—and I let out the most primal noises. Noises that shocked me and took me to an edge where I felt I couldn't go on any longer. I was transitioning. Becoming someone new.

Author and holistic nutritionist Carly Mendes says, "There is a phase in labor, appropriately called transition, where a woman will meet her breaking point. She'll feel as though she just can't go on, and she is right. The maiden in her is not strong enough for the task at hand. It's during this time the maiden dies so that the woman can be reborn as a mother, with her child. A new, more capable version of herself with far more strength than she has ever known. From maiden to mother."[7]

Right after I pushed River out and her cord was unwrapped from her neck, RR caught her and handed our baby to me. I heard my baby cry, sounds of life coming from my nearly eight-pound wide-eyed baby girl, I said three words.

"We did it."

"My baby. We did it."

I think the words we say to ourselves and to our baby right after we meet one another are powerful and unique to each birth. We are in our most powerful, raw state being truest to who we are. Since we're completely new, those first words we speak mark the beginning of something new and special and Divine. We don't plan what we say. It just happens. "We did it" were mine. And those words stamp a reflection of not only believing that I couldn't do it for the entirety of my pregnancy, but a brand-new beginning because I did.

I had done the thing I didn't believe I could do. I made it through to the other side. I proved myself wrong. I knew what I was made of.

Death is a common thing to worry about during pregnancy. Maybe it's because women, especially women of color don't get the care we deserve in hospitals and the maternal and infant death rate in America is embarrassingly high. Maybe it's because we know that as sacred and beautiful and natural and simple as birth is, it isn't the safest thing we will ever do. And it's the first time we know we will give our own lives to save our babies. We are taken to the edge of ourselves, and we will never return the same.

Whatever it is, there's no mistake that we think about death when we are about to give birth. Death is a part of life and we, Americans, have gone to extreme lengths to avoid, not just dying, but even the topic of death. Perhaps birth is the only thing powerful enough to bring us to that edge where we face our deepest fears.

Because truly, to become someone new, something in us must die.

RR, as he watched me push our baby out, said three words too, "There she is."

Intellectually, I know he was talking about our baby, seeing her for the first time, and recognizing that this little girl was real. And there she was. But spiritually, I like to believe he was also talking about me. Watching the power that brought his daughter earthside.

"There she is."

Because there I was. The woman I had been all along but forgotten. I re-membered myself. And he got to bear witness to the re-membering. All the fear I carried for ten months melted away as I sat up in my hospital bed with my baby on my chest. We did it—my baby girl and I. We fought so hard for that moment. To meet each other and know everything was going to be okay.

There is this blissful golden moment where time stands still right after a woman pushes out her baby. Those birth hormones that make a new mama feel high took over my body, and I realized the only thing that could have possibly set me free from all the fear was the very thing I feared the most. Birth. Dying in birth. Losing myself.

In many ways, I did die. It wasn't my last breath in the way we typically think about death. But I became someone totally new. The girl who never fit in with the Country Club Christians, the baseball wife who never seemed to get the rules just right, and the woman who didn't know who she was outside of the labels others put on her was gone.

In those moments as I pushed out my precious baby, I welcomed two new lives into this world. My newborn baby. And myself, a newborn mother. I had seen the darkness in my own life; I had felt the sting of loss, of pain, and of fear. I saw the darkest corners of the world and interacted with women and girls who experienced some of the worst humans imaginable and came out the other side stronger. Just as those girls at Nai Asha had to learn who they were and reconnect with their bodies and their souls, so did I. I was more than the labels others put on me, and I was more than my trauma, pain, and fears. I was a warrior. And I was a mother to two miracles. In those moments, I finally claimed my rebel soul, and embraced who I truly am.

What I thought was my death was actually my dawn. And you know what comes after dawn. An awakening.

* * *

Hope is dangerous. It's wild. It's unpredictable, uncontrollable, and un-limitable. Sometimes our hopes are dashed or delayed, and so we try to run as far as we can in the opposite direction. If we don't get our hopes up, we can't be disappointed, right? But hope is what all of life and good-ness stems from. When we plant a seed in the ground, we have hope that in a few days or a week a sprout will emerge. And we know that sprout will turn into a flower with a bloom. We gaze in awe over the flower. We pick them and decorate our homes with them. We spend all our time amazed at the flower. But let us not forget that the only possible way we obtain the beauty of the flower is by having hope in the darkness of the soil to bring forth new life. It is in darkness that new life is formed.

Hope is undefeatable; it will always rise from the ashes. And when we stop running from it, it will find us and bring us home.

ACKNOWLEDGMENTS

Renu,

Your life touched me and shaped me in ways I'll never be able to explain. Thank you for teaching me how to have hope, even when life feels hopeless.

Ally Fallon,

You took what was brewing in my heart and brain and helped me pour it out onto notecards on your living room floor. For the first time, I saw my book laid out and believed that it was possible. You have remained a constant cheerleader, guiding me through the book writing and pitching process.

Thank you for being the first person in the literary world to believe in me as a writer. Without you, there is no *Dangerous Hope*.

Annie Kyle,

Thank you for challenging and encouraging me as a writer. You were patient with me as I went through each stage of the writing process. You not only made me a better writer, but you also allowed me to believe in myself. You helped me believe I could pitch to dream agents. Your steadiness and encouragement allowed me to get through the tough parts of the publishing world, and stick to writing Dangerous Hope as a love letter to my readers.

To Esther,

You were a breath of fresh air after many disappointing conversations with agents. Your belief in my work as a first-time author and your confidence in signing me as your client means the world. Thank you for representing me, this book, and whatever the future might hold.

The entire Fedd team,

(Danielle, Tori, Ashley, Deryn & Brittney), Wow. You all have made the process of publishing this book enjoyable, smooth, and such a joy. Thank you for giving me the freedom to be creative, decisive, and curious, and for working hard to make this book what it has become.

The M108 Board,

You are the reason we are able to serve a community of vulnerable people across the world. You inspire me. You give me life. You give me hope. My desire is that this book opens the door for more opportunities for Mission 108. Your selfless dedication to the work of anti-trafficking goes unseen by many. Thank you for throwing starfish back into the ocean with me.

Lastly, to my husband Robbie,

It is not easy being married to a woman like me, a writer, a creative, slightly anxious melodramatic person, an Enneagram Four that lives in her head and heart, and needs to be reminded daily to live in her body.

When it didn't seem like there would ever be a single good thing that could come out of my darkest years, you were patient and still with me.

When I wasn't certain if I could pull myself out of the dark depression of losing our babies, you were steady. You are the reason there was space for me to evolve into a woman who could turn her pain into purpose.

Thank you for being my constant support, stability, best friend, and husband.

ABOUT THE AUTHOR

BRITTANY ROSS IS A BUSINESS OWNER, professional suitcase packer, certified yoga teacher, dreamer, and author. She is the CEO and founder of the anti-human trafficking nonprofit, Mission 108, which runs a safe home in India for girls rescued out of sex trafficking.

Brittany came into the public eye early on in her life as the wife of Major League Baseball player Robbie Ross. She and her husband Robbie share their fun-loving and playful life and marriage on Instagram stories. A voice on marriage, motherhood, baseball, and anti-trafficking, Brittany brings her nontraditional perspectives, rebellious soul, messy curls, and huge heart to everything she does.

She grew up in Kentucky, where she was one of the only biracial girls in her neighborhood, with a single mom who shaped her into the open minded, free-thinking storyteller she has become today. She embraces being different and empowers women to own their stories by telling the truth.

Brittany lives in Lexington, Kentucky with her husband, Robbie, and their two girls, Gypsy and River.

ENDNOTES

1   Hillsong Worship, "You'll Come," recorded July 2008, track 14 on *This Is Our God (Live)*, Hillsong Music & Resources, compact disc.

2   Linda Kay Klein, *Pure: Inside the Evangelical Movement That Shamed a Generation of Young Women and How I Broke Free* (New York: Atria Paperback, 2019).

3   Megan Leonhardt, "Women Are Traveling Far and Wide for Affordable IVF-Here's Why It's so Expensive," CNBC (CNBC, August 13, 2019), https://www.cnbc.com/2019/08/13/women-are-traveling-far-and-wide-for-affordable-ivf.html.

4   Christine Richmond, "Random Panic Attacks: Here's What Happens to Your Body," WebMD, November 13, 2021, https://www.webmd.com/anxiety-panic/panic-attack-happening.

5   Shani Jay, "What Is a Moon Circle & How to Host One: Sacred Sisterhood & Magic," She Rose Revolution, accessed June 16, 2022, https://sheroserevolution.com/shanijay/what-is-a-moon-circle/.

6   Layne Redmond, *When the Drummers Were Women: A Spiritual History of Rhythm* (New York: Three Rivers Press, 1997).

7   Carley Mendes, "Transition," Transition | Pregnancy & Birth, 2019, https://pathwaystofamilywellness.org/Pregnancy-Birth/transition.html.